CONTENTS

VIVA L'ITALIA!

I absolutely love Italy, I just can't get enough of it, and in the pages that follow you'll find my ultimate in Italian recipes, each of which delivers big on flavour and comfort, helping you to create food that will definitely make you feel happy. This is about getting right to the heart of the Italian kitchen and, frankly, celebrating the utter joy of great Italian food. What an absolute pleasure.

In Italy, one thing that remains wonderfully consistent is that everyone is incredibly passionate about food. It has always been openly celebrated as being for everyone, and put at the heart of all that Italians do. Importantly, no matter how rich or poor, most Italians eat very well indeed – simple, beautiful, achievable food is standard. Adopting the Italian attitude – an undeniable obsession with seasonal ingredients, a frugal approach to shopping, straightforward common-sense cooking and a little of the magic stuff, love – will serve you well on the path to cooking some of the most spectacular meals to enjoy with family and friends.

I want you to think of this as your go-to Italian book, a manual of deliciousness that you can dip into any day of the week. The recipes are a real mix of fast and slow cooking, familiar classics as well as new things I've learnt, and simple everyday dishes alongside more fantastical, indulgent, labour-of-love options for weekends and those moments when you've got more time to invest in your cooking. There's a reason why Italian food is celebrated the world over, and this book will help you to create that authentic vibe at home, where the aromas as you cook and the tastes when you tuck in will transport you straight to the landscapes of Italy. Whether you've been before or not, I hope to inspire you to visit this great country yourself.

I've been lucky enough to visit Italy many times over the last 25 years, and during that period I've seen, learnt, tasted and quaffed many wonderful things. But I've also noticed a shift in Italian food culture. The time-honoured traditions and recipes of the true matriarchs of the kitchen, the nonnas and mammas who are the beating heart of the Italian home, are at risk of being lost. The incredible heritage that has been passed down from generation to generation is dying out as time passes, lives get busier and technology makes it easier to cut corners. With that in mind, I want to show you just how easy cooking great Italian food can be.

So, over the last two years, I've been back travelling around Italy, where there's always so much to discover, meeting nonnas and mammas, many of whom have been cooking for well over 50 years. I've had the honour of cooking with these wonderful women, and learning some of their secrets. Everyone I met on this journey wanted to share their much-treasured recipes and advice with me so that, in turn, I could pass it all on to you and keep their traditions alive.

Whether it's recipe principles, flavour combinations, tips or techniques, I've absorbed all this incredible insight in order to share with you the true soul of Italian food, to inspire you to experience their traditions and culture yourself, but also to express fresh, totally achievable recipes in an accessible modern way.

On a personal note, I also wanted to seize the opportunity to travel to Italy with my dear best friend and mentor, Gennaro Contaldo, one of the true gentlemen you see on the dedication page of this book. Gennaro has been the driving force behind my love of all things Italian since I met him at Antonio Carluccio's Neal Street restaurant back in the 90s, and it was deeply important for me to have Gennaro at my side on this journey, helping me to connect with the people we met, creating new memories together, and generally causing utter culinary chaos!

So please, sit back, relax, turn the pages, and I hope you find plenty of inspiration to tempt you into the kitchen to get cooking, Italian style.

ANTIPASTI

ANTIPASTI PLANK

Antipasti is the norm in Italy, and is basically an endless array of bits and pieces that you would eat before tucking into your pasta course. The joy of antipasti is making sure you're always riffing off seasonal and local produce, as well as amazing jarred stuff that's been preserved earlier in the year. I like to think of it as Italy's version of a table picnic, and while I'm sure many people will have an opinion on what's right and wrong, for me it's about celebrating what's available to you, and what's great. It's about hunting out the best of the best when it comes to your ingredients, and having fun.

PERFECT FOR SHARING

A good plank is about contrast, not only visually with colour, but also with flavour, texture and even temperature. Think sweet fruit, salty cured meat, bitter greens, soft focaccia, crunchy music bread, cool creamy burrata, hot toast, pecorino and pickles. Put your plank together with joy and common sense, focusing on combinations that just work well together. From veggies to meat to fish to nuts – you get the idea. Invest in a large wooden board or plank to serve up your spread, and sit it high on a few tins, a stack of books, or even a few bricks. It's a laugh, interactive and a great talking point.

ANCHOVIES ON TOAST

WONDERFUL FENNEL, CHILLI & LEMON

~~~~~~

I want to show you how much of a joy fresh anchovies are with this beautiful dish. In this ingenious method, we're going to grill them on toast so we retain all those incredible flavour-packed oils that leach out as they cook. Try this once, and you'll never look back. Fresh sardines would also work an absolute treat here.

SERVES 4–6 | 25 MINUTES

18 fresh whole anchovies (or 8–12 fresh whole sardines)

1 heaped teaspoon fennel seeds

1 big pinch of dried red chilli flakes

1 lemon

olive oil

1 small flat round rustic loaf or ciabatta

optional: fresh fennel tops

Pinch off the anchovy heads, allowing you to quickly scrape out the innards. Pat dry with kitchen paper, then use your thumb and forefinger to push open each anchovy. Pull the spine completely away from the fillets, which in turn lets you butterfly them out flat, and remove the tails. Place the anchovies in a shallow bowl, sprinkle over the fennel seeds and chilli flakes, finely grate over half the lemon zest, squeeze over half the juice, add 2 tablespoons of oil and gently toss together with your fingertips.

Preheat the grill to high. Use a serrated knife to carefully slice the base, then the top, off your loaf, leaving you with a spongy 2cm-thick round (use the offcuts to make breadcrumbs for future meals). Rub the inside of a cold frying pan with a little oil, put in the bread, then, with pride, arrange the dressed anchovies skin side up on top, overlapping and double layering, if needed. Drizzle over any leftover dressing. Press down on the anchovies, pushing them into the bread so they'll cook into each other.

Put the pan on a high heat for 4 minutes to crisp up the base, then place under the grill for just 2 minutes (4 minutes for sardines) to crisp up the top, too. Season to perfection, pick over some fennel tops if you've got them, then slice and serve with lemon wedges. Have a bite, and be happy.

CALORIES	FAT	SAT FAT	PROTEIN	CARBS	SUGAR	SALT	FIBRE
309kcal	12.2g	2g	16.2g	35.6g	2.2g	0.7g	2.2g

OOZY RISOTTO BALLS

SUPPLÌ AL TELEFONO STUFFED WITH MOZZARELLA

When you tear these balls in half you get a long strand of mozzarella and everyone shouts 'supplì al telefono', referring to it looking like a telephone wire, hence the funny name. I've been single-minded here and only filled these delicate little balls with oozy mozzarella, but you can totally pimp your ride by adding a pinch of dried chilli or fresh herbs, a little anchovy, pesto, mushroom, pepper or even another complementary cheese.

SERVES 8 | 1 HOUR 10 MINUTES

½ x White risotto
  (see page 148)

200g plain flour

200g fine stale breadcrumbs

2 large eggs

1 whole nutmeg, for grating

125g ball of mozzarella cheese

50g Parmesan cheese

1 litre sunflower oil, for frying

1 lemon

Make the White risotto (see page 148) the night before you need it, but don't loosen it with extra stock, just add butter and Parmesan, so your risotto is firm enough to form balls. Cool it quickly and keep it in the fridge overnight. The next day, get three shallow bowls and place the flour in one, the breadcrumbs in the second and crack the eggs into the third. Finely grate a few scrapings of nutmeg into the eggs, season, and beat well.

Cut the mozzarella into 24 small chunks. Finely grate the Parmesan and stir it through the cold risotto, then, with wet hands, take a golfball-sized piece and squash the centre with your finger. Place a mozzarella cube in the middle, then shape the rice around it to create a little oval. Roll in flour, dip in egg, let any excess drip off, then turn in the breadcrumbs until evenly coated. Repeat with the remaining ingredients – I like to have helpers and put one person in charge of each bowl.

Pour the sunflower oil into a large, sturdy pan on a medium-high heat and leave to get up to 160°C on a thermometer. Working in batches, carefully lower a quarter of the balls into the hot oil to cook for 7 minutes – this should ensure they're crisp and golden on the outside and wonderfully gooey in the middle. Transfer to a plate lined with kitchen paper to drain, then let the oil come back up to temperature before cooking the next batch. Delicious served with a squeeze of lemon and a cold beer.

CALORIES	FAT	SAT FAT	PROTEIN	CARBS	SUGAR	SALT	FIBRE
518kcal	29.4g	8g	16g	48.9g	2.1g	1.1g	1.7g

SPRING SOUFFLÉ

CREAMY MIXED-CHEESE SAUCE

~~~~~~

There's a big French influence on Torinese cooking. I had the opportunity to cook a classic soufflé with Baronessa Susanna, a lovely lady who's passionate about the flexibility and versatility of dishes like this (although her grandkids love her to just use peas!). I wanted to embrace seasonal veg here, just like Susanna does, but I've also simplified and lightened the recipe. It's a great starter or simple lunch.

SERVES 6 | 1 HOUR 20 MINUTES

1 onion

1 firm courgette

olive oil

1 bunch of asparagus (350g)

3 sprigs of fresh mint

100g freshly podded peas

100ml Pinot Bianco
   white wine

6 large eggs

SAUCE

20g unsalted butter,
   plus extra for greasing

30g plain flour

500ml semi-skimmed milk

100g Parmesan cheese

1 whole nutmeg, for grating

100g Toma, fontina or
   Taleggio cheese

Peel the onion, then finely chop with the courgette. Place in a large frying pan on a medium-high heat with 2 tablespoons of oil. Cook for 10 minutes, stirring occasionally, while you snap off and discard the woody ends of the asparagus, then, reserving a few spears, trim and finely slice the rest. Pick and finely chop the mint leaves. Stir the mint and sliced asparagus into the pan, with the peas and wine. Cook for 10 more minutes, or until soft. Halve the reserved spears lengthways and blanch in boiling salted water for 2 minutes, then drain. Preheat the oven to 180°C.

Meanwhile, for the sauce, melt the butter in a pan on a medium heat. Stir in the flour until combined, then gradually whisk in the milk until smooth. Simmer gently for 5 minutes. Finely grate in most of the Parmesan and nutmeg, crumble in the Toma, then taste and season to perfection. Pour half the sauce into the veg pan and mash together, then leave the mixture to cool to room temperature. Put the remaining sauce aside for now.

Separate the eggs, stirring the yolks into the veg pan. Beat the whites until stiff, then fold through the veg mixture. Generously butter three small–medium heatproof baking dishes, then divide up the soufflé mix, sitting the blanched asparagus on top. Finely grate over the remaining Parmesan, then bake for 15 minutes, or until golden and puffed up. Warm up the remaining cheese sauce, and serve on the side for pouring over.

CALORIES	FAT	SAT FAT	PROTEIN	CARBS	SUGAR	SALT	FIBRE
391kcal	25.8g	11.6g	24.6g	14.4g	8.4g	1g	1.7g

FISH CRUDO

DELICATE, RAW & SUPER-FRESH

~~~~~~

SERVES 6 | 1 HOUR

SEA BASS Finely slice **2 sea bass fillets** (skin off, pin-boned) and arrange on a serving plate. Deseed and finely chop **½–1 fresh red chilli**, scatter over with a pinch of sea salt from a height, then drizzle with **mild extra virgin olive oil**. Very finely chop some **apple**, toss with the juice of **1 lemon** and sprinkle over, drizzling over the excess juice. Leave for 10 minutes, or until the colour changes. Finish with **fresh fennel fronds**.

FRESH ANCHOVIES Prep **10–12 fresh whole anchovies** (see page 14). Squeeze the juice of **1 lemon** on to a serving plate, drizzle with **mild extra virgin olive oil**, and season lightly with sea salt. Pick, finely slice and scatter over the leaves from a few sprigs of **fresh flat-leaf parsley**, then dip and swipe each anchovy through the dressing, arranging them around the plate, silver side up. Drizzle with a little extra oil, to serve.

RED MULLET At an angle ½cm apart, slice **2 red mullet fillets** (scaled, pin-boned) and arrange on a serving plate. Finely grate over the zest of **½ a lemon**, squeeze over all the juice, and leave for 10 minutes, or until the colour changes. Pod a few **fresh peas** and scatter over the top of the mullet with a little **wild rocket**. In the picture, just for fun I placed the fillets back on the fish head and tail to tell the story, but you can serve up as you please. Finish with a drizzle of **mild extra virgin olive oil** and a pinch of sea salt from a height.

BREAM Finely slice **2 bream fillet**s (scaled, pin-boned) and arrange on a serving plate. Quarter and add a few **ripe cherry tomatoes**, then squeeze over the juice of **1 lemon** and leave for 10 minutes, or until the colour changes. Pick over a few **fresh baby basil leaves**, then season and drizzle with **mild extra virgin olive oil**.

TIGER PRAWNS Finely chop **4 large raw tiger prawns** (peeled, deveined) on a board. Finely grate over the zest of **¼ of an orange** and squeeze over ¼ of the juice along with the juice of **½ a lemon**, season with sea salt and black pepper, then mix and pile in the centre of a serving plate. Peel and devein another **6 prawns** and arrange around the plate, squeeze over the rest of the orange and lemon juice, and leave for 15 to 20 minutes, or until the colour changes. Finish with a drizzle of **mild extra virgin olive oil**, a sprinkling of **fresh herb flowers** and some **dried red chilli flakes**. Langoustines are delicious thrown into the mix, too.

CALORIES	FAT	SAT FAT	PROTEIN	CARBS	SUGAR	SALT	FIBRE
225kcal	12.5g	1.8g	25.6g	2.6g	2.1g	1.5g	0.6g

SPRING BRUSCHETTA

SMASHED RAW ASPARAGUS, RICOTTA, FRESH BASIL & PARMESAN

Come springtime, asparagus is one of the first vegetables to poke its head out of the ground, and young, fresh asparagus is so sweet, perfumed and nutritious – it's a joy. There's nothing more beautiful than celebrating it raw, smashing it up to create a wonderful bruschetta topping that will go down a treat at any time of day.

SERVES 6 | 30 MINUTES

1 bunch of asparagus (350g)

1 bunch of fresh basil (30g)

2 lemons

50g Parmesan cheese, plus extra to serve

250g quality ricotta cheese

cold-pressed new season's extra virgin olive oil

6 slices of rye or sourdough bread

1 clove of garlic

Snap off and discard the woody ends of the asparagus, then use a speed-peeler to strip off some nice cross-section ribbons from each spear. Snap the remainder into a large pestle and mortar with a pinch of sea salt. Pick the baby basil leaves and put aside, then pick the rest of the leaves into the mortar. Pound it all into a pulp, then muddle in the juice of half a lemon. Finely grate in the Parmesan and mix in the ricotta (transfer it to a bowl at this stage, if too full), followed by 1 tablespoon of oil. Taste, and season to perfection with black pepper.

Toast the bread in a hot griddle pan until crisp and golden. Halve the garlic clove and lightly rub the cut sides over the toasts, then drizzle lightly with oil. Back spoon on the ricotta mixture, then sprinkle the asparagus ribbons and baby basil leaves on top. Finely shave over a little extra Parmesan, and serve with lemon wedges, for squeezing over.

CALORIES	FAT	SAT FAT	PROTEIN	CARBS	SUGAR	SALT	FIBRE
250kcal	11.3g	5.1g	13g	25.5g	3.1g	1g	2.2g

MOUNTAIN OMELETTE

OOZY ALPINE CHEESES, HAM & CHILLI JAM

I'm in love with this exquisitely delicate omelette. Vigorously but easily made, you simply roll up the thin, blond omelette around melting cheeses and wafer-thin ham with a splash of chilli jam, then slide it straight on to some delicious hot toast. It's a delicious breakfast, brunch, lunch or, even better, late-night snack. It can be simple and everyday, or complex and artisanal – its success is down to the cheeses you buy and the ratio in which you mix them. I've suggested Italian cheeses here, but feel free to swap in great British cheeses, too.

SERVES 1–2 | 5 MINUTES

1 thick slice of rye bread

2 large eggs

30g mixed melty cheeses, such as Toma Valdostana, Toma di Gressoney, fontina, Parmesan

2 slices of wafer-thin ham

1–2 teaspoons chilli jam

1 small knob of unsalted butter

extra virgin olive oil

Put your bread on to toast. Place a 30cm non-stick frying pan on a medium-high heat. In a mug, whip the eggs with a pinch of sea salt and black pepper. Coarsely grate the cheeses. Get your ham and chilli jam ready.

Place the butter in the pan and as soon as it sizzles – within seconds – pour the eggs into the pan and gently swirl around two or three times to cover the base. Sprinkle over the cheese, lay over the ham and flick over the chilli jam. By the time you've done that, the omelette will be cooked.

Tilt and angle the pan, and use a rubber spatula to ease and roll the omelette down the pan, folding it in at the sides halfway down and rolling again so you end up with lots of layers of blond omelette, oozy cheese and ham (don't worry about technique – frantically flip it around and you'll get there). Slide and turn the omelette on to the toast, drizzle with extra virgin olive oil and enjoy that moment of wonderful heaven.

CALORIES	FAT	SAT FAT	PROTEIN	CARBS	SUGAR	SALT	FIBRE
562kcal	38.2g	15.6g	30.7g	26.6g	4.6g	2.7g	2.3g

RAFANATA

BAKED POTATO CAKE OF HORSERADISH, PANCETTA & PECORINO

Rafanata gets its name from 'rafano', which means horseradish and is the key ingredient in this delightful dish. Slice and serve it up as a nibble or as part of an aperitivo spread, or I really like it as a side to any grilled or roasted meat. Served with a simple fresh herb salad, it makes a fantastic lunch for four lucky people.

SERVES 8-12 | 1 HOUR 20 MINUTES

600g potatoes

2 knobs of unsalted butter

semi-skimmed milk

50g pecorino or Parmesan cheese

5cm fresh horseradish, plus extra to serve

3 large eggs

100g piece of smoked pancetta

100g coarse stale breadcrumbs

Peel the potatoes, chop into big even chunks, then cook in a pan of boiling salted water for 15 to 20 minutes, or until tender. Drain and leave to steam dry for 2 minutes, then return to the pan. Add 1 knob of butter and a splash of milk, finely grate in the cheese and peeled horseradish and crack in the eggs. Mash and mix well, season to perfection, then put aside.

Preheat the oven to 200°C. Slice the pancetta and place in a cold 18cm non-stick ovenproof frying pan. Place the pan on a medium heat and when the pancetta starts to sizzle, add the breadcrumbs. Toss over the heat until crisp and golden, then mix into the mash pan.

Now, press the mash into the frying pan, smoothing it out with a slight curve. Fry on a medium heat for 5 minutes, jiggling the pan to create a nice rounded edge. Loosen the edges with a spatula, then lift slightly and pop the remaining knob of butter into the pan underneath. Once melted, put a plate on top of the pan, carefully flip over, and slip the rafanata back into the pan. Bake in the oven for 30 minutes, or until golden and hot through. Serve with extra horseradish finely grated over the top, to taste.

CALORIES	FAT	SAT FAT	PROTEIN	CARBS	SUGAR	SALT	FIBRE
227kcal	13g	6g	9.2g	20g	1.4g	1g	1.6g

TUNA CARPACCIO

SMOKY CHILLI, CAPER & OREGANO DRESSING

The time to make this exciting dish is when your fishmonger has a chunk of amazingly fresh tuna that's clearly optimal quality and deep in colour. Searing the outside gives contrast and texture, while the dressing cuts through the richness of the raw fish and has wonderful layers of flavour. Everyone will thank you for it.

SERVES 6 | 30 MINUTES

2 tablespoons baby capers
  in brine

3 fresh mixed-colour chillies

1 tablespoon dried oregano,
  ideally the flowering kind

500g piece of super-fresh
  yellowfin tuna

olive oil

2 lemons

extra virgin olive oil

1 clove of garlic

4 anchovy fillets in oil

1 teaspoon fennel seeds

100g ripe mixed-colour cherry
  tomatoes

20g wild rocket

Soak the capers in a bowl of water. Prick the chillies, blacken all over on the flame of a gas hob, then place in a bowl and cover with clingfilm. Sprinkle the oregano and a pinch of sea salt and black pepper over the tuna from a height and pat it all over, then drizzle with 1 tablespoon of olive oil. Sear the tuna in a hot frying pan on a high heat for just 30 seconds on each side (including the edges), then remove to a board.

Drain the capers, return them to the bowl, squeeze over the juice from 1½ lemons and drizzle with 2 tablespoons of extra virgin olive oil. Peel, finely chop and add the garlic, then finely slice and add the anchovies, along with the fennel seeds. Scrape the blackened skin off the chillies, tear them open, deseed, then finely slice lengthways and gently mix in.

Slice the tuna as finely as you can and lay over a large serving platter or divide between six plates. Spoon over the dressing, then quarter the tomatoes and scatter over with the rocket. Serve right away, with lemon wedges on the side for squeezing over.

CALORIES	FAT	SAT FAT	PROTEIN	CARBS	SUGAR	SALT	FIBRE
156kcal	7.1g	1.1g	22.1g	1.1g	1g	0.9g	0.4g

SWISS CHARD CHIPS

WHIPPED RICOTTA, CHILLI DUST & ANCHOVIES

I have to say that cooking greens until crispy like this is not an Italian technique, but the principle of dressing beautifully blanched greens with good oil and seasoning definitely is. This recipe came about after I left a batch of greens near my wood oven and thus created an incredibly delicious mistake and a lovely handheld receptacle that, when filled with a little beaten ricotta, chilli and anchovies, people just go mad for.

SERVES 12 | 45 MINUTES

24 medium-sized Swiss chard leaves

olive oil

50g Parmesan cheese

1 lemon

250g quality ricotta cheese

extra virgin olive oil

6 anchovy fillets in oil

1 teaspoon dried red chilli flakes

Preheat the oven to 150°C. Trim just the tough ends off the chard stalks, then wash the leaves well. Pat dry with kitchen paper, then drizzle with 3 tablespoons of olive oil, season with sea salt and toss with your fingertips, making sure every single leaf is well dressed. Lay across baking trays in a single layer, with no overlaps – this will ensure that each leaf gets wonderfully crisp. Roast for 20 minutes, or until crisp – use your instincts.

Meanwhile, finely grate the Parmesan and half the lemon zest into a bowl, then squeeze in half the juice. Add the ricotta and 2 tablespoons of extra virgin olive oil, and mash it all up with a fork. Taste and season to perfection with a little salt and black pepper. Drain the anchovies, finely slice them lengthways and dress with the remaining lemon juice. Pound the chilli flakes in a pestle and mortar until super-fine.

Serve each crispy chard leaf with a spoonful of whipped ricotta, a strip of anchovy and a pinch of chilli dust. Fold, roll, crunch and enjoy.

CALORIES	FAT	SAT FAT	PROTEIN	CARBS	SUGAR	SALT	FIBRE
117kcal	9.1g	3g	5.7g	3.6g	1.1g	1g	0g

FLAKY FISH FRITTERS

COD, SMOKED MOZZARELLA, CAPERS, PARSLEY & LEMON

I love fishcakes and fritters and often, across Italy and the Mediterranean, salt cod is used – it's wonderful but can be quite hard to find here in the UK. So with that in mind, I've developed a simple technique that can be done quickly and successfully, creating delicious flaky-textured cod at home, with ease.

SERVES 6 | 50 MINUTES, PLUS SALTING

200g skinless, boneless cod

100g rock salt

500g potatoes

½ a bunch of fresh flat-leaf parsley (15g)

25g baby capers in brine

75g scamorza (smoked mozzarella cheese)

25g Parmesan cheese

100g fine stale breadcrumbs

1 large egg

sunflower oil, for frying

2 lemons

In a bowl, cover the cod with the rock salt, then cover and refrigerate for 1 hour. Meanwhile, peel and roughly chop the potatoes, cook in a pan of boiling water for 15 minutes, or until tender, then drain, mash and cool.

When the time's up, rinse the cod under cold running water to remove the salt and pat dry. Chop half into ½cm cubes, then finely chop the rest and place it all in a large bowl. Pick the parsley leaves and finely chop with the capers, then chop the scamorza into 1cm cubes and add it all to the cod. Finely grate in the Parmesan and add the breadcrumbs and cooled potato. Season with black pepper, crack in the egg, then mix everything together well. Now shape the fritters however you like – use wet hands to make 18 balls or patties, or use two tablespoons to shape into 18 oval quenelles.

When you're ready to cook, pour 1cm of sunflower oil into a large, sturdy, shallow pan on a medium-high heat. Once hot, place half the fritters in the oil to cook for 1 to 2 minutes on each side, or until golden and crisp. Transfer to a plate lined with kitchen paper to drain while you get on with the second batch. Serve with lemon wedges, for squeezing over.

CALORIES	FAT	SAT FAT	PROTEIN	CARBS	SUGAR	SALT	FIBRE
347kcal	22.4g	3.1g	14.6g	23.1g	1.3g	1g	1.4g

ROSE VEAL TARTARE

DELICATELY DRESSED WITH FENNEL, CAPERS, CHILLI & HERBS

This fantastic starter or fun lunch is incredibly delicious, easy to digest, exciting and, for most people, a bit of a treat. Veal works brilliantly as an alternative to beef – it's light, lean and a great carrier of flavours.

SERVES 2 | 20 MINUTES

1 tablespoon baby capers in brine

200g rose veal fillet

50g piece of lardo

1 shallot

¼ of a bulb of fennel

2 sprigs of fresh flat-leaf parsley

1 lemon

¼ teaspoon dried red chilli flakes

4 anchovy fillets in oil

cold-pressed extra virgin olive oil

1 large egg

Soak the capers in a bowl of water. On a large board, use a large sharp knife to chop the rose veal and lardo as finely as you can. Peel and very finely chop the shallot. Trim and very finely chop the fennel, including any leafy tops, and the parsley leaves. Finely grate half the lemon zest. Pound the chilli flakes in a pestle and mortar until fine.

Now, drain the capers and add to the board with the chilli flakes and anchovies. Chop and mix it all together, tweaking with drips of lemon juice and up to 1 tablespoon of oil until you get the seasoning spot on. Spoon on to a pretty plate, then separate the egg (save the white for another recipe), sitting the yolk in the middle.

To devour, simply mix the yolk through the tartare and tuck on in. Serve with music bread, grissini or hot grilled ciabatta, and a wedge of lemon.

CALORIES	FAT	SAT FAT	PROTEIN	CARBS	SUGAR	SALT	FIBRE
322kcal	21.3g	6.1g	30.6g	2.2g	1.6g	1.4g	0.3g

OCTOPUS SALAMI

SPIKED WITH CHILLI, FENNEL SEEDS & PARSLEY

When octopus is fresh, seasonal to you locally, and a good price, this cool recipe is an utter joy and a delightful thing to make from scratch. Ask your fishmonger to give you around 2kg of octopus in total – whether that's one large or two smaller ones, it doesn't matter, just adjust the cooking time accordingly, and have fun!

SERVES 8 | 50 MINUTES, PLUS CHILLING OVERNIGHT

1 large octopus (2kg), cleaned, beak removed

olive oil

2 cloves of garlic

2 fresh red chillies

250g ripe cherry tomatoes

1 tablespoon fennel seeds

1 bunch of fresh flat-leaf parsley (30g)

350ml Sicilian white wine

1 lemon

50g wild rocket

1 orange

Plunge the octopus into a very large, deep pan of boiling water (no salt – this is very important!) for 2 minutes to clean it, then lift out on to a large plate (it will curl up slightly). Pour the water away, then place the pan back on a medium heat with 10 tablespoons of oil. Return the octopus to the pan and cook for 5 minutes, while you peel the garlic and finely slice it with 1 chilli, and halve the tomatoes. Throw the garlic, chilli and tomatoes into the pan with the fennel seeds and parsley (stalks and all), then pour over the wine. Cover and simmer for 35 minutes, or until tender (depending on its size – smaller ones won't need as long). Turn the heat off, and leave until cool enough to handle, but still warm.

On a flat surface, lay out a double layer of clingfilm to create a 50cm square. Lift the octopus out of the pan with tongs, shaking to drain away the excess liquid, then place in the middle of the clingfilm. Our objective is to make an octopus sausage, so fold the clingfilm over the octopus, then roll it up as tightly as you can, being careful not to trap the clingfilm inside, and pushing out the air as you go. Pinch and squeeze the ends, pushing the octopus right into the centre and compacting it well, then twist and tie a knot at each end to seal. Place the parcel on another double layer of clingfilm and repeat the process as tightly as you can. Place in the fridge for at least 24 hours, then use a sharp knife to slice it into ½cm-thick rounds through the clingfilm. Peel off the clingfilm, and serve with lemon-dressed rocket, sliced chilli and a grating of orange zest.

CALORIES	FAT	SAT FAT	PROTEIN	CARBS	SUGAR	SALT	FIBRE
393kcal	19.8g	3.1g	45.7g	1.7g	1.5g	0.1g	0.8g

MOZZARELLA FRIED EGGS

SWEET TOMATOES, FRESH BASIL & TOAST

This is the most fantastic starter or brunch. It's so easy to put together, and perfect placed in the middle of the table ready to share with friends and family. The way the mozzarella melts into the tomatoes creates the most wonderfully tasty casing for the eggs as they cook, which is just divine. You'll love tucking into this one.

SERVES 4-6 | 15 MINUTES

1 dried red chilli

1 clove of garlic

olive oil

2 sprigs of fresh basil

6 ripe mixed-colour tomatoes

125g ball of mozzarella cheese

6 large eggs

4–6 slices of sourdough bread

Deseed the chilli and tear it into a large cold frying pan. Peel and finely slice the garlic, add with 4 tablespoons of oil, and place the pan on a medium heat. Season with sea salt and black pepper, tear in the basil leaves and let it all fry for around 1 minute while you randomly chop up the tomatoes.

As soon as everything starts to sizzle, throw the tomatoes into the pan, then, a couple of minutes later, tear in the mozzarella. Making little gaps, crack in the eggs. Cover, then cook for 3 to 5 minutes, or until the eggs are cooked to your liking. Meanwhile, toast the bread. Season the pan of eggs from a height with black pepper, and serve up with the hot toasts.

CALORIES	FAT	SAT FAT	PROTEIN	CARBS	SUGAR	SALT	FIBRE
437kcal	29.5g	8.8g	20.4g	23.9g	4.7g	1.5g	1.8g

CHICKPEA FRITTERS

LEMONY ROSEMARY OIL & ROCKET

I've taken inspiration from the classic farinata, which is more of a flat pancake that uses chickpea flour, and created these delicious but easier-to-make fritters using humble tinned chickpeas. They're fantastic enjoyed as nibbles to share, or even thrown into a warm salad or smashed into a flatbread with other tasty things.

SERVES 8 | 35 MINUTES

2 x 400g tins of chickpeas

3 lemons

2 large eggs

1 teaspoon dried red chilli
   flakes

120g plain flour

1 teaspoon baking powder

olive oil

2 sprigs of fresh rosemary

extra virgin olive oil

50g wild rocket

Drain the chickpeas and tip into a food processor. Finely grate in the zest of 1 lemon and squeeze in its juice, crack in the eggs, add the chilli flakes, flour, baking powder and a really good pinch of sea salt and black pepper, then pulse until just combined – you want to keep a bit of texture.

Put a large non-stick frying pan on a medium-high heat. Once hot, add 2 tablespoons of olive oil. Working in batches, spoon tablespoons of the mixture into the pan (you should end up with 24 in total). Cook each batch for around 10 minutes, turning regularly until golden all over, removing to a plate lined with kitchen paper to drain as they're ready.

Meanwhile, strip the rosemary leaves into a pestle and mortar with a good pinch of salt and pound into a paste. Squeeze in the juice of the remaining lemons, then muddle in the same amount of extra virgin olive oil. When all the fritters are done, reduce the heat under the pan to low and pour in the rosemary dressing for just 30 seconds. Sprinkle the rocket over a platter, pile on the fritters, pour over the dressing, and serve right away.

CALORIES	FAT	SAT FAT	PROTEIN	CARBS	SUGAR	SALT	FIBRE
231kcal	13.3g	2.1g	7.4g	21.5g	0.8g	0.7g	3.4g

SALADS

GRILLED APRICOT SALAD

FLOWERING THYME, MOZZARELLA, PINK PEPPERCORNS & PROSCIUTTO

Years ago, when I first learnt to appreciate the way Italians use fruit in salads, it changed my concept of a salad for good. It took it from a wimpy side dish to a true gastronomic experience. This recipe is about celebrating textures and brightness, and I think you'll love it. You could swap in other seasonal stone fruit.

SERVES 4 | 25 MINUTES

8 ripe apricots

8 sprigs of fresh thyme, ideally the flowering kind

olive oil

2 tablespoons white wine vinegar

extra virgin olive oil

1 big pinch of pink peppercorns

½ a red onion

2 large handfuls of salad leaves, such as escarole, Castelfranco, wild rocket

4 slices of prosciutto

125g ball of mozzarella cheese

1 lemon

Put a griddle pan on a high heat. Halve and destone the apricots then, on a platter, toss with half the thyme sprigs and 1 tablespoon of olive oil. Place the dressed fruit cut side down on the hot griddle for 6 minutes, or until charred and caramelized, turning halfway.

Meanwhile, pour the vinegar on to the platter with 2 tablespoons of extra virgin olive oil. Crush and crumble the pink peppercorns over the platter, then peel, very finely slice and sprinkle over the onion, giving it a little mix in the dressing to lightly pickle it. Pick through your salad leaves, tearing or slicing the larger ones. Add to the platter and gently toss together, then season to perfection. Tear the prosciutto and it drape over in waves.

Gently tear open the mozzarella, season with sea salt, black pepper, a fine grating of lemon zest and a few drips of extra virgin olive oil, then tear over the salad. Place your grilled apricots in and around the salad, sprinkling over any crispy thyme leaves and the remaining leaves and flowers. Drizzle with a tiny bit more extra virgin olive oil, then serve.

CALORIES	FAT	SAT FAT	PROTEIN	CARBS	SUGAR	SALT	FIBRE
244kcal	18.9g	6.3g	10g	9.2g	8.6g	1.3g	1.1g

SMASHED SMOKY AUBERGINE

BABY BROAD BEANS, ALMONDS, HONEY & OREGANO

Something extraordinary happens when you blacken and char the skin of aubergines – the smokiness that process gives to the creamy inside is incredible. Once dressed with good oil, lemon, herbs and other nice things, you get a dish that can be enjoyed as it is, as a dip or antipasto, on pizza, or with pasta or grilled meats.

SERVES 6 | 40 MINUTES

2 large aubergines (400g each)

25g blanched almonds

350g fresh broad beans, in their pods

1 lemon

25g pecorino or Parmesan cheese

extra virgin olive oil

1 teaspoon runny honey

4 sprigs of fresh oregano or marjoram

1 loaf of rustic bread

Prick the aubergines and place directly on the coals of your barbecue, straight on the flame of a gas hob, or under a super-hot grill, turning until blackened and burnt all over (about 15 minutes), then remove to a large board to cool slightly. Meanwhile, bash the almonds in a pestle and mortar until fine. Pod the broad beans, pinching the skins off the larger beans.

Halve the aubergines lengthways and scoop the flesh and juices out on to the board, discarding the burnt skins. Chop the aubergines with the broad beans and almonds, using your knife to keep folding everything back on itself. Squeeze over the lemon juice, finely grate over the pecorino, drizzle with 4 tablespoons of oil and the honey, then chop and mix it all together again. Season to perfection, then pick and tear over the oregano leaves. Serve with hot toasts on the side. Heaven.

CALORIES	FAT	SAT FAT	PROTEIN	CARBS	SUGAR	SALT	FIBRE
329kcal	14g	2.4g	12g	41.6g	6.7g	1.1g	4.6g

SICILIAN ARTICHOKES

BOILED LEMON, HONEY, THYME & PISTACHIOS

Rose Gray and Ruth Rogers showed me a version of this recipe many years ago when I worked at the River Cafe – it completely blew my mind. It's so elegant, so different, and utterly delicious. Since then I've enjoyed it in many different ways, but I particularly love this version with pistachios. Wonderful served as it is, with flatbreads, with prosciutto, other cured meats or boiled ham, with mozzarella or on pizza. Go on, give it a go.

SERVES 4-6 | 1 HOUR 30 MINUTES

2 large unwaxed lemons

12 Italian violet artichokes

½ a clove of garlic

8 sprigs of fresh thyme, ideally the flowering kind

extra virgin olive oil

2 tablespoons runny honey

30g shelled unsalted pistachios

Cook 1 whole lemon in a large pan of boiling salted water for 30 minutes, or until the skin is tender. Reserving the pan of water, remove the lemon to a board to cool. Trim the artichoke stalks 2cm from the base, then add to the lemony water, topping it up, if required. Pop a plate on top to keep them submerged. Cover, bring to the boil, then cook over a medium heat for 10 to 15 minutes, or until tender. Drain and, once cool enough to handle, peel away the outer leaves until you reach the paler ones that are tender enough to eat. Trim the heads to 3cm, then cut in half lengthways. Carefully scoop out and discard the hairy choke from the centre.

Peel the garlic and put into a pestle and mortar with a pinch of sea salt. Strip in half the thyme leaves and bash until fine. Squeeze in half the juice from the raw lemon and muddle in 3 tablespoons of oil to make a dressing.

Halve the boiled lemon lengthways, scoop out and discard the soft inside, then trim away any white pith. Finely slice the tender yellow skin into long, thin strips and scatter over a serving platter with the artichokes. Drizzle over the dressing and honey, squeeze over the remaining raw lemon juice, season to perfection and toss to coat. Pick over the remaining thyme leaves and flowers. Crush and scatter over the pistachios, and serve.

CALORIES	FAT	SAT FAT	PROTEIN	CARBS	SUGAR	SALT	FIBRE
196kcal	13.4g	2g	7.3g	14.8g	11.4g	0.6g	0.7g

MATERA SALAD

ROCKET, MINT, APPLE, CRUNCHY VEG, ORANGE & CHILLI DRESSING

Inspired by the ingredients that kept popping up in the Basilicatan region, I've come up with this beautiful salad recipe. One of the links and foundations is the marinating of the oranges with chilli, which also results in the creation of an incredible dressing that's both punchy and refreshing, like a ray of Italian sunshine.

SERVES 4-6 | 30 MINUTES

1 clove of garlic

3 oranges

1 teaspoon dried red chilli flakes

red wine vinegar

extra virgin olive oil

100g red cabbage

½ a cucumber

6 small mixed-colour heritage carrots

4 sprigs of fresh mint

1 eating apple

50g wild rocket

200g ball of burrata

Halve the garlic clove and rub the cut sides all over a large serving platter. Top and tail the oranges, trim away the peel, cut into rounds and arrange on the platter. In a pestle and mortar, bash the chilli flakes with 1 teaspoon of sea salt until fine, then scatter most of it over the orange slices. Drizzle with 3 tablespoons each of red wine vinegar and oil and leave to marinate.

Meanwhile, very finely shred the cabbage. Peel the cucumber and halve lengthways, removing the seedy core, then chop into small chunks. Wash the carrots and finely slice lengthways. Pick the mint leaves, slicing or tearing the larger ones. Core the apple and slice into thin wedges, then place it all on the platter with the rocket. Season with salt and black pepper, then gently toss together with your fingertips to dress.

Tear open the soft, oozy burrata, place proudly on top of the salad, drizzle with a little more oil, sprinkle over the remaining chilli dust from a height, and serve. Great with a stack of hot toasts on the side.

CALORIES	FAT	SAT FAT	PROTEIN	CARBS	SUGAR	SALT	FIBRE
343kcal	22.4g	8.6g	11.3g	25.9g	23.4g	2.3g	8.7g

AMAZING SWEET PEPPERS

HOT TOASTS & CREAMY BURRATA

In this homage to peppers, which are a real Basilicatan speciality, we focus on bringing out their intense natural sweetness by giving them the time to cook until lovely and soft, then dressing them with fragrant ingredients that really hero their flavour. Served with hot crunchy toasts and creamy burrata, it's glorious.

SERVES 4 | 45 MINUTES

4 teaspoons baby capers
   in brine

4 long mixed-colour peppers

4 cloves of garlic

olive oil

½ a bunch of fresh
   marjoram, oregano or
   summer savory (15g),
   ideally the flowering kind

8 black olives (stone in)

1 lemon

extra virgin olive oil

4 slices of sourdough bread

200g ball of burrata

Soak the capers in a bowl of water. Deseed the peppers and slice into 1cm-thick strips, peel and finely slice the garlic, and place both in a large frying pan on a medium heat with 1 tablespoon of olive oil. Strip in the herb leaves, reserving any flowers. Cook for 30 minutes, or until soft and sweet, stirring regularly and adding splashes of water to stop them sticking, if needed. Meanwhile, squash and destone the olives. Drain the capers, then use a fork to roughly mash them up with the olive flesh.

When the peppers are soft and sticky, reduce the heat to low and spoon in the olive and caper mixture. Squeeze over the lemon juice, drizzle with 1 tablespoon of extra virgin olive oil and mix well. Taste, season to perfection and dot over any reserved herb flowers. Toast the bread.

To serve, tear open the burrata alongside the peppers. Drizzle the burrata with just a little extra virgin olive oil and sprinkle from a height with black pepper. Stack up the toasts, and let people scoop and squash the peppers and burrata on to them as they wish. Gorgeous!

CALORIES	FAT	SAT FAT	PROTEIN	CARBS	SUGAR	SALT	FIBRE
332kcal	18.9g	8.2g	12.8g	28.4g	7.8g	1.6g	4.4g

PANZANELLA

SLOW-ROASTED CHERRY TOMATOES, BASIL & BREAD WITH SEAFOOD SKEWERS

~~~~~~

Panzanella is one of my favourite unconventional salads. In this recipe, the secret ingredient is time – slow-roasting the tomatoes so their flavour leaches into the drying croutons gives you the ultimate base to receive that incredible greenhouse dressing. Teamed with these delicious skewers, it's sure to go down a treat.

SERVES 4 | 2 HOURS 40 MINUTES

1.5kg ripe mixed-colour cherry
  tomatoes, on the vine

300g sourdough bread

red wine vinegar

olive oil

1 bunch of fresh basil (30g)

1 clove of garlic

extra virgin olive oil

50g wild rocket

1 lemon

SKEWERS

300g firm white fish fillets,
  such as hake, skin off,
  pin-boned

8 scallops, shelled, trimmed

4 thick sprigs of fresh
  rosemary, for skewering

8 raw king prawns, shell off,
  deveined

12 rashers of smoked pancetta

Preheat the oven to 100°C. Pick 1kg of tomatoes, prick each one with the tip of a sharp knife, blanch in a pan of boiling salted water for 40 seconds, then drain. Once cool enough to handle, pinch off the skins, placing the tomatoes in your largest roasting tray. Tear in the bread in chunks the same size as the tomatoes. Drizzle with 1 tablespoon each of vinegar and olive oil, and roast low and slow for 2 hours.

Pick the remaining tomatoes into a blender with half the basil leaves. Peel and add the garlic, a pinch of sea salt and 1 tablespoon of vinegar. Blitz until smooth, then pass through a coarse sieve into a large bowl. Add 2 tablespoons of extra virgin olive oil, then taste and season to perfection.

Chop the fish into chunks the same size as the scallops. Strip the leaves off the rosemary sprigs (saving the leaves for another recipe, or use soaked wooden skewers), then divide and skewer up the fish, prawns and scallops. Wrap the pancetta in and around, and place the skewers in a snug-fitting tray. Remove the tomato tray from the oven, turn it up to full whack (240°C), and cook the skewers for 10 minutes, or until golden and just cooked through. Meanwhile, toss the tomatoes and bread in the dressing, and leave to soak. To serve, toss the rocket and remaining basil leaves through the panzanella, plate up, sit the skewers on top, and serve with lemon wedges.

CALORIES	FAT	SAT FAT	PROTEIN	CARBS	SUGAR	SALT	FIBRE
537kcal	18.3g	3.7g	40.4g	53.8g	15.1g	2.3g	6.1g

ARTICHOKE SALAD

LEMON, CAPERS, ROCKET & SALTED RICOTTA

I love this salad – it's confident, simple, delicious and makes a real hero of artichokes, which are held up by classic flavours of the south. I enjoy it as a starter or side salad to accompany whole roasted chicken or fish.

SERVES 6-8 | 1 HOUR

16 Italian violet artichokes

2 lemons, for artichoke prep

SALAD

2 tablespoons baby capers
   in brine

2 lemons

olive oil

1 large clove of garlic

70g wild rocket

extra virgin olive oil

20g salted ricotta or pecorino
   cheese

Pop the capers into a bowl of water to soak while you prep the artichokes (see page 382). When you're done, drain the artichokes well, finely slice them, squeeze over the juice from 2 lemons, then toss well to coat.

Put 2 tablespoons of olive oil into a large cold frying pan, peel, squash and add the whole garlic clove to perfume the oil, drain and add the capers, then place the pan on a medium heat. When everything starts to sizzle, add the lemon-dressed artichokes and toss over the heat for 4 minutes to soften them ever so slightly, yet still retain a good bit of bite.

Tip the artichokes on to a nice serving platter, discarding the garlic clove, and sprinkle over the rocket. Drizzle with a little extra virgin olive oil, shave or finely grate over the cheese, then gently toss together with your fingertips. Season to perfection, if needed, then tuck in.

CALORIES	FAT	SAT FAT	PROTEIN	CARBS	SUGAR	SALT	FIBRE
84kcal	6.2g	1.5g	5g	4g	1.9g	0.5g	0.2g

BABY COURGETTE SALAD

WHIPPED PECORINO RICOTTA & BLACK OLIVE TAPENADE

Enjoying baby courgettes while they're raw and firm, and appreciating their delicateness, crunch and amazing colour, is a joy. We're also celebrating ricotta, and convincing ourselves it's savoury by teaming it with a little pecorino. Finishing with a quick tapenade for contrast in colour and flavour, this is a winning little plateful.

SERVES 6 | 15 MINUTES

1 lemon

cold-pressed extra virgin
   olive oil

12 firm mixed-colour baby
   courgettes, with flowers

2 sprigs of fresh mint

100g black olives (stone in)

250g quality ricotta cheese

25g pecorino or Parmesan
   cheese, plus extra to serve

optional: chive or other herb
   flowers

Squeeze the lemon juice into a bowl, add an equal amount of oil and season with sea salt and black pepper. Halve the smallest courgettes lengthways, leaving any flowers intact. Finely slice the rest at an angle, then place them all on the dressing, ready to toss at the last minute.

Strip the mint leaves into a pestle and mortar and pound well. Squash the olives and remove the stones, adding the flesh to the mortar. Bash to a paste, then muddle in 2 to 3 tablespoons of oil to make a thick tapenade. Place the ricotta in a bowl, finely grate over the pecorino, add a pinch of salt and pepper, then whip up until smooth.

Back spoon and spread a heaped tablespoon of ricotta on to each of your six serving plates. Delicately toss the courgettes in the dressing and pile on to the ricotta, dividing over any leftover dressing from the bowl. Spoon a little olive tapenade over each portion, saving the rest for another day. Finish with a sprinkling of herb flowers, if using, and serve.

CALORIES	FAT	SAT FAT	PROTEIN	CARBS	SUGAR	SALT	FIBRE
178kcal	16.2g	5.3g	6.1g	2g	1.9g	1.4g	0.7g

ROMAN CELERY SALAD

DRESSED WITH SMASHED ANCHOVIES, LEMON, GOOD OIL & CHILLI DUST

A fresh, crunchy, zingy mouthful of joy is what you'll get with this salad, which celebrates a vegetable that has spent most of its career as the bridesmaid, not the bride. Prepping and dressing the celery like this pays homage to this great veg and the dressing really embraces the spirit of Roman flavours. Fantastic served with grilled meat or fish, paired with mozzarella or even stuffed into a flatbread with cured meats and cheese.

SERVES 8 | 25 MINUTES

2 heads of celery

8 anchovy fillets in oil

extra virgin olive oil

1 large lemon

½ teaspoon dried red chilli flakes

Get yourself a large bowl of iced water ready to go. Use a speed-peeler to remove the celery bases and stringy outer edges. Wash well, then very finely slice the heads (yellow leaves and all), with good knife skills, a speed-peeler or on a mandolin (use the guard!). As you go, drop the celery into the iced water so it curls and crisps up beautifully.

In a pestle and mortar, pound the anchovies into a paste, then gradually muddle in 8 tablespoons of extra virgin olive oil and the lemon juice. Drain the celery well, pat dry with a clean tea towel and place in a serving bowl. Drizzle over the dressing and delicately toss with your fingertips until evenly dressed. Clean the pestle and mortar, pound the chilli flakes into a fine dust and, from a height, scatter as much as you dare over the salad.

CALORIES	FAT	SAT FAT	PROTEIN	CARBS	SUGAR	SALT	FIBRE
122kcal	12.3g	1.8g	1.1g	1.7g	1g	0.6g	0.8g

WINTER SALAD

SWEET ROASTED ONIONS, CRUSHED HAZELNUTS & BAROLO DRESSING

Learning to enjoy a range of bitter leaves is a really important part of educating your palate and exploring a whole new dimension of flavours. Instead of thinking about bitter as a negative, we riff off it here by teaming it with the sweetness of roasted onions, the sourness of vinegar and the satisfying crunch of nuts.

SERVES 6-12 | 1 HOUR 20 MINUTES, PLUS COOLING

6 red onions

1 bulb of garlic

½ a bunch of fresh
   thyme (15g)

100g blanched hazelnuts

olive oil

600g mixed bitter leaves,
   such as chicory, radicchio,
   Castelfranco, Treviso,
   dandelions

DRESSING

1 tablespoon Dijon mustard

extra virgin olive oil

50ml Barolo red wine

2 tablespoons red wine
   vinegar

Turn the oven on to full whack (240°C). Place the unpeeled onions in a snug-fitting dish and roast for 1 hour, or until soft and slightly burnt. After 30 minutes, halve the garlic bulb across the middle and add to the dish. Toss the thyme sprigs and hazelnuts in a little olive oil and sprinkle over the onions for the last 5 minutes. Remove and leave to cool.

Trim and separate the bitter leaves (I like to take a bit of pride in this and prep each leaf depending on its size – tear up the big ones, leave the little delicate ones whole, you get the idea). For the dressing, squeeze the roasted garlic into a bowl (discarding the skins) and mash well, then mix in the mustard and a pinch of sea salt. Whisking constantly, drizzle in 6 tablespoons of extra virgin olive oil, then, still whisking, let the dressing down with the Barolo and vinegar.

Squeeze the sweet onions out of their crispy skins into a serving bowl, breaking them up a bit as you go. Season with salt and black pepper, then drizzle over the dressing. Top with the bitter leaves, tossing with your fingertips until beautifully dressed. Crush the hazelnuts in a pestle and mortar until fairly fine, then scatter over the salad.

CALORIES	FAT	SAT FAT	PROTEIN	CARBS	SUGAR	SALT	FIBRE
306kcal	24g	2.8g	5.3g	18.4g	11.5g	0.8g	5.3g

SOUPS

ACQUACOTTA

HUMBLE TUSCAN SOUP

~~~~~~

Acquacotta is a truly ancient dish created by the grafters of the land. It orginates in Maremma, the southern part of Tuscany, and this recipe was a real lifeline, intended to satisfy one's appetite in good times and bad. The engine of the acquacotta is the bread, which is a lightweight, safe, stable, tasty form of energy. It also makes use of the genius deep savouriness of rosemary and a small amount of any dried mushroom, as well as nutty, sweet squash or pumpkin. My family and I really love this super-nutritious veggie recipe.

SERVES 4-6 | 30 MINUTES

1 onion

1 potato

2 sticks of celery

200g squash or pumpkin

olive oil

20g dried porcini mushrooms

2 sprigs of fresh rosemary

1 x 400g tin of quality plum
    tomatoes

200g seasonal greens, such as
    Swiss chard, cavolo nero

4 large eggs

4 large slices of stale
    sourdough bread

pecorino or Parmesan cheese

cold-pressed new season's
    extra virgin olive oil

Peel the onion, potato, celery (reserving any leaves) and squash, then chop into rough 1cm chunks – there's no need to be precise. Place a large pan on a medium heat with 2 tablespoons of olive oil and the chopped veg. Cook for 10 minutes, or until softened but not coloured, stirring occasionally.

Stir the porcini, rosemary sprigs, 2 litres of water, and a good pinch of sea salt and black pepper into the pan. Bring to the boil, then scrunch in the tomatoes through your clean hands. Simmer for 10 minutes while you prep the greens. Remove the tough stalks, finely slicing and adding any that are tender enough to eat, then roughly shred the leaves. Pick out and discard the rosemary sprigs, stir in the greens, and cook for 5 minutes.

At this point, have a slurp and correct the seasoning. Now, simply crack the eggs into the soup as spaced out as your pan allows. Cover and poach to your liking. Meanwhile, toast the bread, then divide between large, warm soup bowls. Ladle over the veg, broth and eggs. Finish with a fine grating of cheese and a lovely drizzle of extra virgin olive oil, then sprinkle over any reserved celery leaves. The toast will suck up all that flavoursome broth and become wonderfully soft and delicious. Yum.

CALORIES	FAT	SAT FAT	PROTEIN	CARBS	SUGAR	SALT	FIBRE
345kcal	15.3g	2.9g	15.1g	38.8g	10.6g	1.5g	4.7g

BORLOTTI BEAN SOUP

FRAGRANT ROSEMARY OIL & TOAST

Making you feel happy and replete with every mouthful, this is a deeply delicious soup. Yes, it's frumpy and not the prettiest bowlful, but that's the point, no ego! It's humble, nutritious, tasty and cheap to make. The ingredients are simple, and adding rosemary oil at the end is a real game-changer, taking it to the next level.

SERVES 6-8 | 2 HOURS, PLUS SOAKING OVERNIGHT

500g dried borlotti beans

2 litres quality chicken or
  veg stock

6 cloves of garlic

2 onions

1 large potato

1 ripe plum tomato

6 sprigs of fresh rosemary

cold-pressed extra virgin
  olive oil

1 teaspoon red wine vinegar

6–8 slices of sourdough bread

Overnight, soak the beans in plenty of cold water. The next day, drain them and place in a big pan. Pour in the stock and enough water to cover the beans by 5cm, then place on a medium heat. Peel 4 cloves of garlic, the onions and potato, then add them all to the pan whole with the tomato. Simmer gently for 1 to 2 hours, or until the beans are super-soft, creamy and almost falling apart, stirring occasionally (the cooking time will vary depending on how old your beans are, so keep checking). Meanwhile, quickly flash the rosemary under hot water, then strip the leaves into a pestle and mortar. Pound into a smooth paste with a pinch of sea salt, then muddle in enough oil to loosen and put aside.

When the beans are ready, scoop the onions, garlic, potato and tomato on to a board and use a large knife to carefully chop to a mush. Stir back through the soup. Simmer to your desired consistency, then stir through 8 tablespoons of oil and the vinegar. Season to perfection, then keep the soup on the lowest heat while you toast the bread. Halve the remaining garlic cloves, rub the cut sides over the toasts and divide between warm bowls. Ladle over the soup, and finish with the rosemary oil.

CALORIES	FAT	SAT FAT	PROTEIN	CARBS	SUGAR	SALT	FIBRE
626kcal	18.6g	2.8g	32.4g	82.9g	7.2g	1.1g	23.3g

MINESTRONE

RISOTTO RICE & SEASONAL VEG WITH PARMESAN, LEMON & GARLIC PESTO

~~~~~~

I love this minestrone – it feels fresh and electric with the contrasting pesto, while the risotto rice sucks up all the incredible flavour and is extremely comforting. Minestrone has always felt like a wonderful fallback recipe – from my days as a student to being a busy parent, I love reacting to what's available at the market, growing in the garden, or even the odds and ends hiding in the veg drawer, to create a beautiful bowl of soup.

SERVES 6-8 | 1 HOUR 10 MINUTES

2 onions

2 sticks of celery

olive oil

600g mixed green veg, such
   as courgettes, fennel,
   tenderstem broccoli,
   asparagus, chard, kale,
   peas, broad beans

200g Arborio risotto rice

2 litres quality chicken or
   veg stock

1 mixed bunch of fresh
   rosemary & thyme (30g)

2 cloves of garlic

50g Parmesan cheese

1 lemon

extra virgin olive oil

Peel the onions and celery, then finely chop both and place in a large pan on a medium heat with 2 tablespoons of olive oil. Cook for 15 minutes, stirring occasionally. This is a good time to prep your green veg, chopping courgettes and fennel into ½cm chunks, and finely slicing broccoli, asparagus, chard and kale. Put the veg aside. Stir the rice into the pan for 2 minutes, then pour in the stock. Tie the herbs together and add to the pan. Bring to the boil, then simmer gently for 15 minutes.

Meanwhile, peel the garlic and pound into a paste in a pestle and mortar with a pinch of sea salt. Finely grate in the Parmesan and lemon zest, squeeze in the juice, and muddle in 4 tablespoons of extra virgin olive oil.

Stir the veg into the soup and simmer for a final 10 to 15 minutes, ensuring that the veggies retain their vibrancy. Season to perfection, then divide between warm bowls. Finish with spoonfuls of the pesto.

CALORIES	FAT	SAT FAT	PROTEIN	CARBS	SUGAR	SALT	FIBRE
324kcal	13g	3.4g	16.8g	36.9g	6.3g	0.9g	3.7g

MUSHROOM BREAD SOUP

OREGANO, STINGING NETTLES, PORCINI & CHILLI FLAKES

This is one of my favourite soups, embracing the incredible depth of flavour you can achieve with mixed mushrooms. Simmered with wild greens, then teamed with stale bread, they make a thick, comforting soup that can even be served on a platter. Wonderfully, if you have leftovers, the soup almost tastes better the day after you've made it, when all those flavours have mingled even more. This dish is one to make you smile.

SERVES 6 | 40 MINUTES

20g dried porcini mushrooms

2 onions

2 cloves of garlic

olive oil

30g unsalted butter

½ teaspoon dried red chilli flakes

½ a bunch of fresh oregano (15g)

600g mixed mushrooms

100g stinging nettles, borage, spinach or rocket

300g stale sourdough bread

extra virgin olive oil

optional: pecorino or Parmesan cheese, to serve

In a jug, cover the porcini with 1.2 litres of boiling kettle water. Peel and finely chop the onions and garlic, then soften in your widest pan on a medium-high heat with 1 tablespoon of olive oil, the butter and chilli flakes for 5 minutes. Strip in the oregano leaves, then stir regularly while you trim the mushrooms, tearing or slicing any larger ones so they're all a pleasure to eat. Stir into the pan and cook for 5 minutes, then add the greens, followed by the porcini and soaking water (discarding just the last gritty bit). Bring to the boil, then let it bubble away for 15 minutes.

Tear the bread into bite-sized chunks and stir into the pan with 2 tablespoons of extra virgin olive oil. As soon as the bread sucks up that lovely broth, it's ready. Taste and season to perfection with sea salt and black pepper, then dish up. Serve with a fine grating of cheese, if you like.

CALORIES	FAT	SAT FAT	PROTEIN	CARBS	SUGAR	SALT	FIBRE
266kcal	11.7g	3.7g	8g	32.5g	5g	0.6g	3.5g

CHICKPEA & BROAD BEAN SOUP

CHILLI OIL, MYRTLE & WALNUT PESTO

Myrtle pesto is outrageously delicious – it's hard to find myrtle in supermarkets, but you can get it at the garden centre and it grows a treat in the UK. Go out of your way to find jarred, fat chickpeas – it's worth it.

SERVES 6 | 1 HOUR

4 dried red chillies

olive oil

1 red onion

1 carrot

½ a celery heart

1 courgette

1 x 700g jar of chickpeas

350g fresh broad beans, in their pods

200g stale sourdough bread

1 x Myrtle & walnut pesto (see page 377)

Tear the chillies in half, shake out and discard the seeds, then place the chillies in a large, sturdy pan on a low heat with 10 tablespoons of oil. Toast for 2 minutes to crisp them up and let them impart flavour into the oil, then pour into a bowl, leaving 1 tablespoon of the oil in the pan.

Peel the onion, carrot and celery, then chop with the courgette to about the same size as the chickpeas, adding to the pan as you go. Turn the heat up to medium and cook for 15 minutes, stirring occasionally. Meanwhile, pod the broad beans, pinching away the skin from any larger beans.

Stir the beans into the pan with the chickpeas (juice and all), and 3 jars' worth of water. Simmer on a medium heat for 15 minutes. Tear the bread into small bite-sized chunks, stir into the soup, then turn the heat off and let it sit for 15 minutes, whereupon you can season it to perfection with sea salt and black pepper. Meanwhile, make your pesto (see page 377). Use a fork to crush up the chillies in the cool oil.

Serve the soup in warm bowls with dollops of pesto and a drizzle of chilli oil (saving any leftover pesto and chilli oil for another day).

CALORIES	FAT	SAT FAT	PROTEIN	CARBS	SUGAR	SALT	FIBRE
382kcal	23.2g	3.7g	12.5g	31.5g	9.5g	0.7g	8.1g

STRACCIATELLA

GREEN VEG, SAFFRON & SILKY EGGS

This is the most wonderful, humble, comforting soup, which you can tailor to reflect the season by tweaking the fresh veg you choose to add to the mix. Bound together with clouds of silky tender Parmesan eggs, this is food to make you feel good. You need to invest in good-quality chicken stock for the best results, or, even better, use homemade broth or meat stock, ensuring maximum flavour from that beautiful bowlful.

SERVES 4 | 20 MINUTES

40g Parmesan cheese

1 whole nutmeg, for grating

2 tablespoons fine semolina

4 large eggs

4 large chard leaves

½ a bunch of asparagus (175g)

1 litre quality chicken stock

20g dried porcini mushrooms

100g freshly podded peas

1 pinch of saffron

extra virgin olive oil

Finely grate the Parmesan and half the nutmeg into a bowl, then add the semolina and crack in the eggs. Season and whisk together. Finely slice the chard stalks and tear up the leaves. Snap off and discard the woody ends of the asparagus. Slice the stalks at an angle, leaving the tips whole.

Warm the stock in a pan on a medium heat, adding the porcini to rehydrate. Drop in the peas, chard, asparagus and saffron, and bring to a gentle simmer. The most common method in Italy is to whisk the broth as you add the eggs, giving you tiny curds of egg and a cloudy, but tasty, broth. I prefer to gently pour the eggs into the broth and simply leave them to cook through for a couple of minutes, so the broth remains clear and elegant, and you get beautiful big curds and sheets of silky egg that you can break up yourself when you tuck in. Ladle into your bowls, finish with a little drizzle of oil, and serve.

CALORIES	FAT	SAT FAT	PROTEIN	CARBS	SUGAR	SALT	FIBRE
253kcal	12.7g	4.4g	23.2g	13.1g	2.4g	1.4g	3.1g

TUSCAN SOUP

SAUSAGE, FENNEL SEEDS, BREAD, BEANS & VEG

Viva la zuppa Toscana! All that veg, propped up by the delicious flavour of quality sausage (choose Italian, if you can), and the really subtle hum of chilli in the background, plus the potatoes, beans and bread sucking up all the goodness – this soup has got it all. It's a bit like the feral cousin of a classic ribollita. You'll love it.

SERVES 8-10 | 1 HOUR

4 quality sausages (300g total)

olive oil

2 teaspoons fennel seeds

½ teaspoon dried red chilli flakes

2 onions

2 sticks of celery

2 carrots

2 potatoes

1 x 700g jar of white beans

200g cavolo nero or kale

200g stale sourdough bread

extra virgin olive oil

optional: Parmesan cheese

Squeeze the sausagemeat out of the skins into a large casserole pan on a medium heat with 1 tablespoon of olive oil, the fennel seeds and chilli flakes. Fry for 5 minutes, or until golden, breaking up the sausage with a wooden spoon. Meanwhile, peel and roughly chop the onions, celery, carrots and potatoes. Stir into the pan and cook on a low heat for 15 minutes, or until softened, stirring occasionally. Pour in the beans (juice and all), then cover with 1.5 litres of water and bring to the boil. Tear the stalks out of the cavolo nero and discard, then roughly slice the leaves and stir into the pan. Tear in the bread into bite-sized chunks. Simmer gently for 30 minutes, or until the soup is wonderfully thick.

Stir in 200ml of extra virgin olive oil, then season the soup to perfection with sea salt and black pepper. Divide between warm bowls and tuck in. Nice finished with a little grating of Parmesan, if you like.

CALORIES	FAT	SAT FAT	PROTEIN	CARBS	SUGAR	SALT	FIBRE
490kcal	33.1g	6.4g	14.3g	35g	5.9g	1g	5.3g

CACIO E PEPE

SPAGHETTI, BLACK PEPPER, BUTTER & PECORINO

Using just four ingredients that work together to create an epic combination, this is a classic, humble and simple Roman pasta. It's recently become one of the most trendy pasta plates to order on the London and New York restaurant scenes, and while some chefs like to make it slightly silky, the classic is a little drier in texture, like mine – you can adjust it to your own preference. Finely cracking black peppercorns yourself is non-negotiable if you want to get this dish right, as is investing in a suitably tangy pecorino. Don't be fooled by the minimal ingredients – there's real subtlety in the detail, and that's what makes it so special.

SERVES 4 | 15 MINUTES

300g dried spaghetti

2 teaspoons black peppercorns

80g good pecorino cheese

1 knob of unsalted butter

Cook the pasta in a pan of boiling salted water according to the packet instructions. As it cooks, briefly toast the peppercorns in a dry frying pan, then crack and pound in a pestle and mortar until nice and fine. Pass through a sieve, discarding anything left behind. Grate the pecorino as super-finely as you can – this helps it melt in an even way, without it clumping together, which can happen if it's grated too coarsely or if it's added while the pan is too hot.

When the pasta's cooked, place the frying pan back over the lowest heat, sprinkle in most of the pepper and add the butter. Once melted, use tongs to drag the pasta straight into the frying pan, letting some starchy cooking water go with it. Take the pan off the heat, sprinkle over three-quarters of the cheese, then leave to sit – without stirring – for 1 minute. Now, without using tongs or a wooden spoon, simply toss it all together, then divide and serve, finishing with the last bit of pecorino and pepper. Delicious served with a green salad and some cold white wine – happy days!

CALORIES	FAT	SAT FAT	PROTEIN	CARBS	SUGAR	SALT	FIBRE
371kcal	12.1g	6.9g	13.6g	55.6g	2.5g	0.9g	2.2g

STROZZAPRETI

MINI MEATBALLS & BAKED CHERRY TOMATO SAUCE

This is a truly delicious pasta that people will never forget. You do invest a little time in slow-roasting the cherry tomatoes, but the immense flavour you get in return is hard to ignore. This one is easy to double up.

SERVES 4 | 1 HOUR 30 MINUTES

1kg ripe mixed-colour cherry tomatoes

3 cloves of garlic

2 fresh bay leaves

olive oil

white wine vinegar

1 red onion

15g raisins

15g pine nuts

250g minced pork shoulder

50g stale breadcrumbs

2 sprigs of fresh mint

300g dried strozzapreti or penne pasta

25g pecorino or Parmesan cheese

extra virgin olive oil

Preheat the oven to 190°C. Prick each tomato with the tip of a sharp knife, blanch in a pan of boiling salted water for 40 seconds, then drain. Once cool enough to handle, pinch off the skins, placing the tomatoes in a roasting tray. Peel, roughly chop and add the garlic, throw in the bay leaves, drizzle with 1 tablespoon of olive oil and a swig of vinegar, season with sea salt and black pepper and toss to coat. Roast for 30 minutes, or until starting to caramelize. Meanwhile, peel and very finely slice the onion, then place in a large frying pan on a medium heat with 1 tablespoon of olive oil. Roughly chop and add the raisins, then season. Cook gently for 15 minutes, or until softened, stirring regularly. Crumble in the pine nuts for the last few minutes, then remove from the heat and leave to cool.

Put the pork, breadcrumbs and cooled onion mixture into a bowl. Pick, finely chop and add the mint leaves, then season. Scrunch and mix together, then, with wet hands, roll into 16 balls, just slightly bigger than the tomatoes. Fry the balls in 1 tablespoon of olive oil in the large frying pan on a medium-high heat for 5 minutes, or until golden all over, jiggling the pan regularly. Spoon into the tomato tray and bake for 20 minutes.

Meanwhile, cook the pasta in a pan of boiling salted water according to the packet instructions, then drain, reserving a mugful of starchy cooking water. Use two spoons to gently toss the pasta into the tray of balls, loosening with a little reserved cooking water. Finely grate in the pecorino, gently toss again, then drizzle with extra virgin olive oil. Yum.

CALORIES	FAT	SAT FAT	PROTEIN	CARBS	SUGAR	SALT	FIBRE
637kcal	26.6g	6.5g	26.8g	77.6g	17.1g	1.6g	6.5g

CLASSIC CARBONARA

CRUNCHY PORCINI BREADCRUMBS

While this is one of the most famous Roman pastas, actually ham, eggs, cheese and pasta is a combination that's been celebrated for a long time throughout all of Italy. There's much debate about the perfect carbonara, but sourcing guanciale, going heavy on the pepper and cracking it fresh, as well as controlling the temperature of your pan, are what's key to this fantastic, comforting pasta. I love the classic recipe I've given you here, but with the bolt-on of crunchy porcini breadcrumbs it just eats so well, plus it's a nice evolution and surprise.

SERVES 4 | 30 MINUTES

80g piece of guanciale (cured pig's cheek) or smoked pancetta

10g dried porcini mushrooms

2 sprigs of fresh rosemary

80g stale rustic bread

½ tablespoon black peppercorns

300g dried spaghetti or bucatini

2 large eggs

50g Parmesan cheese

Trim off and roughly chop the guanciale skin, then place just the skin in a blender with the porcini. Strip in the rosemary leaves, tear in the bread and blitz into rough crumbs. Toast in a large dry frying pan on a medium heat until golden, tossing regularly. Tip into a bowl for later. In the same pan, briefly toast the peppercorns, then crack and pound in a pestle and mortar until fine. Pass through a sieve, discarding anything left behind. Remove the frying pan from the heat for a few minutes to cool slightly.

Cook the pasta in a pan of boiling salted water according to the packet instructions. Meanwhile, chop the guanciale into ½cm chunks, sprinkle into the frying pan with the pepper, and place on a medium-low heat until the fat has rendered out and turned golden. In a bowl, beat the eggs, then finely grate in most of the Parmesan and beat again.

Using tongs, drag the pasta straight into the guanciale pan, letting some starchy cooking water go with it to break the frying. Toss with all that gorgeous flavour, then remove from the heat and – of utmost importance – wait 2 minutes for the pan to cool before adding the eggs (if it's too hot, they'll scramble; get it right and they'll be smooth, silky and elegant). Moving the pasta, toss in the eggs, loosening with extra cooking water, if needed. Plate up immediately, finely grate over the remaining Parmesan and serve with the golden breadcrumbs, for sprinkling.

CALORIES	FAT	SAT FAT	PROTEIN	CARBS	SUGAR	SALT	FIBRE
475kcal	15g	5.7g	23g	66.5g	3.3g	1.4g	3g

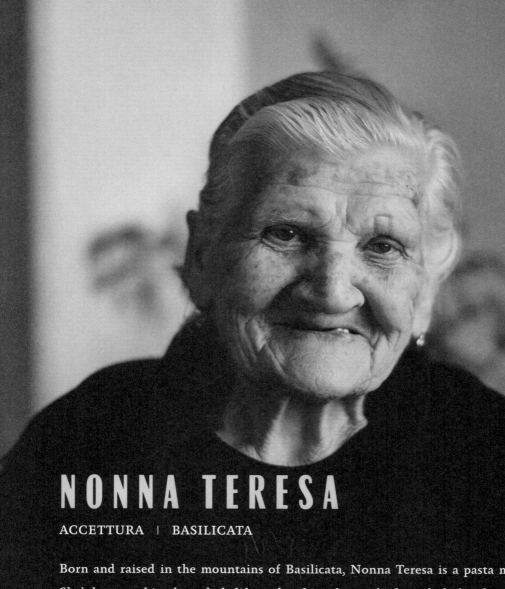

NONNA TERESA

ACCETTURA | BASILICATA

Born and raised in the mountains of Basilicata, Nonna Teresa is a pasta maestro. She's been cooking her whole life, and making dinner for her whole family since the age of 7, when she had to have food ready for her parents as they returned from a day working the fields. Teresa told me it wasn't until she was 15 years old that she got her first pair of shoes. That's something that I just don't think we can get our heads around now – it really puts into perspective the meaning of 'cucina povera' (poor cooking). Every ingredient Teresa and her family had was so important, and she is incredibly adept at making a small amount of ingredients go a long way. Her clever cooking is delightful, and I feel so privileged I got to share a meal with her.

NONNA TERESA'S PASTA

CRISPY HORSERADISH & CHILLI BREADCRUMBS

A good pangrattato (flavoured crispy breadcrumbs) has the ability to add not only flavour, but also incredible texture to a meal. The use of horseradish here is very unusual, yet very delicious and makes total sense as it was one of the few vegetables growing locally to Teresa. Dishes like this respect the scarcity of ingredients.

SERVES 4 | 15 MINUTES

300g dried bucatini or
  rigatoni

olive oil

50g coarse stale breadcrumbs

1 teaspoon dried red chilli
  flakes

5cm fresh horseradish

2 cloves of garlic

½ a bunch of fresh thyme
  (15g)

2 dried red peppers
  (see page 226) or
  8 sun-dried tomatoes

extra virgin olive oil

Cook the pasta in a pan of boiling salted water according to the packet instructions, then drain, reserving a mugful of starchy cooking water.

Meanwhile, for the pangrattato, put 2 tablespoons of olive oil into a large frying pan on a medium-high heat with the breadcrumbs and chilli flakes. Peel and finely grate in the horseradish, then fry for 5 minutes, or until crisp, stirring regularly. Tip into a bowl and put aside. Return the frying pan to a medium heat with 2 tablespoons of olive oil. Peel, finely slice and add the garlic, strip in the thyme leaves, then tear in the dried peppers, discarding the seeds. Fry for just 1 minute, then toss in the drained pasta, loosening with a little reserved cooking water, if needed. Season to perfection, divide between warm bowls, drizzle lightly with extra virgin olive oil and generously sprinkle over the pangrattato.

CALORIES	FAT	SAT FAT	PROTEIN	CARBS	SUGAR	SALT	FIBRE
498kcal	23.5g	3.2g	11.1g	64.5g	3.7g	0.5g	2.8g

SQUID SPAGHETTI

MUSSELS, PARSLEY, WHITE WINE, CHILLI & SQUID INK

~~~~~~

This is a really fun, simple, visually exciting and incredibly tasty pasta. It's quick to make, and with a nice cold glass of white wine on the side it's a joy to share with someone special. You should be able to get squid ink in good supermarkets or from your fishmonger, but if not you'll find it's just one click away online.

SERVES 2 | 15 MINUTES

250g mussels, scrubbed, debearded

150g dried spaghetti

2 cloves of garlic

¼ of an onion

½ a fresh red chilli

olive oil

2 anchovy fillets in oil

100g baby squid, cleaned

100ml Greco di Tufo white wine

2 teaspoons squid or cuttlefish ink

½ a bunch of fresh flat-leaf parsley (15g)

cold-pressed extra virgin olive oil

Pick through the mussels and tap any that are open – if they don't close, discard. Cook the pasta in a pan of boiling salted water according to the packet instructions. Meanwhile, peel and finely chop the garlic and onion, finely slice the chilli and place it all in a large frying pan on a high heat with 2 tablespoons of olive oil and the anchovies. Fry, stirring regularly, while you finely slice the squid into rings, keeping the tentacles whole. Stir the wine and squid ink into the pan and let it reduce by half. Add all the squid and the mussels, pop the lid on and leave for 3 to 4 minutes, or until the mussels have opened (discard any that remain closed).

Meanwhile, pick and roughly chop the parsley leaves. Once cooked, use tongs to drag the pasta straight into the frying pan, letting some starchy cooking water go with it. Sprinkle in the parsley, then toss over the heat for 1 minute, loosening with an extra splash of cooking water, if needed. Dish up, drizzle with a little extra virgin olive oil, and tuck right in.

CALORIES	FAT	SAT FAT	PROTEIN	CARBS	SUGAR	SALT	FIBRE
510kcal	20.6g	3g	24.7g	60.3g	4.1g	0.8g	3g

PISTACHIO PASTA

RAW GARLIC, TOMATO, HERB & LEMON SAUCE

When produce is good and abundant, it's a complete pleasure to embrace ingredients in their raw state. This gives you a sauce that sings with the hum of garlic, the sweetness of ripe tomatoes, the fragrance of fresh herbs, that wonderful zing from the lemon and, most importantly, that moreish crunch yet wonderful softness from the savoury, luminous green pistachios. It's said that the best pistachios grow on the side of Mount Etna, if you're lucky enough to visit. For me, this easy Sicilian-inspired dish is an absolute delight.

SERVES 4 | 20 MINUTES

50g shelled unsalted pistachios

300g dried spaghetti

1 clove of garlic

1 lemon

50g pecorino or Parmesan cheese

extra virgin olive oil

½ a bunch of fresh oregano (15g)

1 bunch of fresh flat-leaf parsley (30g)

400g ripe mixed-colour tomatoes

Pound the pistachios to dust in a pestle and mortar, then put aside. Cook the pasta in a pan of boiling salted water according to the packet instructions. Meanwhile, peel and finely chop the garlic. Sprinkle with a pinch of sea salt, then make a paste by crushing the salt into the garlic with the side of your knife. Scrape into a large bowl, finely grate in the lemon zest and pecorino, squeeze in the lemon juice, and add 4 tablespoons of oil. Pick, finely chop and add the herb leaves. Chop the tomatoes into rough 1cm chunks, add to the bowl and toss everything together with your fingertips, then taste and season to absolute perfection.

When the pasta's done, use tongs to carefully drag it straight into the bowl of sauce, letting a little starchy cooking water go with it. Toss until well coated, loosening with a little extra cooking water, if needed. Divide between your bowls, sprinkle over the pistachio dust, and devour.

CALORIES	FAT	SAT FAT	PROTEIN	CARBS	SUGAR	SALT	FIBRE
512kcal	24.6g	5.5g	15.6g	60.7g	6.6g	1.1g	4.4g

TORTIGLIONI

FRESHLY PODDED PEAS, GUANCIALE, MINT & PECORINO

This is a celebration of delicious, sweet peas and is proper comfort food. It's super-simple and quick to put together, and the beautiful sweetness of the peas is contrasted brilliantly by the salty depth of flavour from the guanciale. Pecorino is the Roman cheese of choice, made with sheep's milk, and worth hunting out.

SERVES 2 | 25 MINUTES

350g fresh peas, in their pods

80g piece of guanciale
(cured pig's cheek)
or smoked pancetta

150g dried tortiglioni or
rigatoni

2 shallots

½ a lemon

½ a bunch of fresh mint (15g)

30g pecorino cheese, plus
extra to serve

extra virgin olive oil

optional: pea shoots, to serve

Pod the peas and place just the pods in a pan of boiling salted water for 5 minutes to impart their flavour. Finely dice the guanciale, place in a large cold non-stick frying pan and put on a medium heat to render the fat, tossing regularly. Meanwhile, scoop out and discard the pea pods, then cook the pasta in the boiling salted water according to the packet instructions. Peel and rustically chop the shallots, then add to the guanciale pan for 5 minutes, or until lightly golden. Add the peas and a good splash of water, then finely grate in the lemon zest. Cover and cook gently for 5 minutes, tossing occasionally, while you rip the top leafy half off the mint and finely chop it, and finely grate the pecorino.

Drain the pasta, reserving a mugful of starchy cooking water. Pour the pasta into the frying pan, then remove from the heat and toss well so the pasta absorbs maximum flavour. Stir in the mint and pecorino, jiggling the pan to create creaminess. Loosen with a little cooking water, if needed, season to perfection, then serve with an extra grating of pecorino, a kiss of extra virgin olive oil, a squeeze of lemon, and a few pea shoots, if you like.

CALORIES	FAT	SAT FAT	PROTEIN	CARBS	SUGAR	SALT	FIBRE
622kcal	23.1g	9.1g	32g	76.6g	7.3g	2.2g	11.9g

ASPARAGUS LINGUINE

COOKED UNTIL SILKY WITH BUTTER, PECORINO & A TOUCH OF CHILLI

I learnt this technique for cooking asparagus from one of the nonnas I met at the market in Rome. By frying, then adding a little liquid and reducing to a low temperature, you ensure the flavours combine beautifully. Creating emulsification at the very end gives a perfect sauce that's as much about flavour as it is texture.

SERVES 4 | 15 MINUTES

300g dried linguine

300g mixed asparagus
  (wild, white, regular)

4 cloves of garlic

2 dried red chillies

olive oil

1 knob of unsalted butter

30g pecorino or Parmesan
  cheese, plus extra to serve

1 lemon

Cook the pasta in a pan of boiling salted water according to the packet instructions. Meanwhile, snap off and discard the woody ends of the asparagus, then finely slice the spears at an angle, leaving the tips whole. Peel and finely slice the garlic, crumble up the dried chillies, and place both in a large frying pan on a medium heat with 2 tablespoons of oil and the butter. When the garlic starts to sizzle, stir in the asparagus. Let it start to fry, then add a spoonful of pasta water, cover, and leave to simmer on a low heat until the pasta is al dente.

Using tongs, drag the pasta straight into the asparagus pan, letting a little starchy cooking water go with it. Turn the heat off, then finely grate in the pecorino and toss together until the fat, cheese and liquid make a natural creamy sauce – loosen with a little extra cooking water, if needed. Taste and season to perfection, then divide between your plates. Finish with a grating of pecorino and a little lemon zest, to taste.

CALORIES	FAT	SAT FAT	PROTEIN	CARBS	SUGAR	SALT	FIBRE
407kcal	15g	5.3g	13.3g	58.3g	4.1g	0.3g	2.2g

SAUSAGE STRACCI

SQUASH, BAY, BLACK PEPPER & PARMESAN

Stracci means 'tatty' – beautifully uneven, silky, erratic little handkerchiefs that can embrace many different sauces. Come autumn, the single-mindedness and simplicity of these ingredients, slowly fried for maximum flavour, create the most exquisite comfort food. Sausage, squash, the hum of pepper and floral bay – delicious.

SERVES 4 | 40 MINUTES

½ x Royal pasta dough
 (see page 370)

olive oil

8 fresh bay leaves

4 quality sausages (300g total)

1 onion

1 stick of celery

300g butternut squash

1 tablespoon red wine vinegar

50g Parmesan cheese

cold-pressed new season's
 extra virgin olive oil

Start by making your Royal pasta dough (see page 370). Put 2 tablespoons of olive oil and the bay leaves into a large cold frying pan. Squeeze the sausagemeat out of the skins into the pan and break apart with a wooden spoon. Place the pan on a medium heat so the fat renders out, then fry until lightly golden, stirring occasionally. Meanwhile, peel the onion and celery, then chop them with the squash, finely but not uniformly. Stir into the pan with a generous pinch of black pepper. Cook for 15 to 20 minutes, or until soft and lightly coloured – take your time. When done, season with a little sea salt, then stir in the vinegar and let it cook away.

Roll out your pasta dough to 2mm thick, then cut or tear it into erratic 5cm shapes. Drop the pasta into a large pan of boiling salted water for just 2 minutes, then use a slotted spoon to scoop it straight into the frying pan, letting some starchy cooking water go with it. Finely grate over most of the Parmesan, drizzle with extra virgin olive oil, then toss together and let the sauce emulsify. Plate up, then finely grate over the remaining Parmesan and finish with a light drizzle of extra virgin olive oil.

CALORIES	FAT	SAT FAT	PROTEIN	CARBS	SUGAR	SALT	FIBRE
741kcal	44g	13.6g	34g	53.4g	7.6g	1.8g	4.3g

BUCATINI AMATRICIANA

GUANCIALE, BLACK PEPPER, ONION, TOMATOES & PECORINO

Although not from Rome originally, this has become one of the city's most famous pasta dishes. It now includes tomatoes, though traditionally it didn't. It's a great pasta sauce that's delicious and simple to make, and pays tribute to guanciale – cured pig's cheek – which you can get in good Italian delis. It's well worth the hassle of finding it, though of course smoked fatty British pancetta or bacon would also be agreeable.

SERVES 2 | 20 MINUTES

80g piece of guanciale (cured pig's cheek) or smoked pancetta

olive oil

150g dried bucatini or spaghetti

1 red onion

1 x 400g tin of quality plum tomatoes

20g pecorino or Parmesan cheese

extra virgin olive oil

Chop the guanciale into rough and ready lardons and place in a large frying pan on a medium heat with 1 tablespoon of olive oil to get golden. Meanwhile, cook the pasta in a pan of boiling salted water according to the packet instructions, then drain, reserving a mugful of starchy cooking water. Peel and finely slice the onion and stir into the guanciale pan with lots of black pepper. Cook for 5 minutes, or until softened, stirring occasionally. Scrunch in the tomatoes through your clean hands, then add a pinch of sea salt and simmer on a low heat until the pasta is ready.

Toss the pasta into the sauce, loosening with a little reserved cooking water, if needed, then season to perfection with more pepper. Divide between warm plates, finely grate over the pecorino and drizzle with a little extra virgin olive oil. It's not traditional, but I sometimes tear over a few fresh basil, thyme or marjoram leaves, to finish.

CALORIES	FAT	SAT FAT	PROTEIN	CARBS	SUGAR	SALT	FIBRE
590kcal	27.3g	8.3g	21.2g	69.6g	15.1g	2.5g	5.6g

PRAWN & TUNA LINGUINE

AGRODOLCE STYLE WITH PISTACHIOS, PARSLEY, VINEGAR & SAFFRON

Inspired by my time cooking with Nonna Rosanna, this sweet and sour pasta is an absolute joy, and uses prawns and their heads for maximum flavour. I'm using her trick of washing sliced onions to make them milder, and that moisture also helps to add extra sweetness as they cook, before we add vinegar for contrast.

SERVES 2 | 45 MINUTES

2 small onions

4 large raw shell-on prawns

olive oil

1 cinnamon stick

2 anchovy fillets in oil

1 good pinch of saffron

4 tablespoons white wine
  vinegar

50g shelled unsalted pistachios

pecorino or Parmesan
  cheese rind

150g dried linguine

200g yellowfin tuna

½ a bunch of fresh flat-leaf
  parsley (15g)

Peel and finely slice the onions, and place them in a bowl of water. Pull off the prawn heads and put just the heads into a cold frying pan with 2 tablespoons of oil and the cinnamon. Place on a medium heat and, once sizzling, add the anchovies. Drain the onions and toss into the pan. Cover and cook for 20 minutes, or until super-soft, stirring occasionally and adding a splash of water, if needed. Meanwhile, peel the prawns, run a small sharp knife down the back of each to butterfly them, then pull out and discard the vein. Steep the saffron in a splash of boiling water and the vinegar. Pound the pistachios in a pestle and mortar. And, for another Rosanna trick, finely grate a little pecorino rind, for seasoning.

Cook the pasta in a pan of boiling salted water according to the packet instructions. Meanwhile, chop the tuna into erratic 1cm chunks, and finely chop the top leafy half of the parsley. With 2 minutes to go on the pasta, remove the lid from the onions and turn the heat to high. Gently squash each prawn head so all the tasty juices spill out into the pan, then discard the heads and the cinnamon. Stir in half the parsley, then break the frying by adding the saffron vinegar mixture. Stir in the prawns and tuna, then use tongs to drag the pasta straight into the pan, letting a little starchy cooking water go with it. Toss over the heat for 2 minutes, loosening with a little extra cooking water, if needed. Turn the heat off, quickly toss in the grated pecorino rind and the pistachios, taste and check the seasoning, then sprinkle over the remaining parsley.

CALORIES	FAT	SAT FAT	PROTEIN	CARBS	SUGAR	SALT	FIBRE
699kcal	29.3g	4.1g	46.4g	66.3g	10.6g	0.6g	6.2g

SAUSAGE CAVATELLI

SWEET & SPICY THYME-SPIKED CHILLI PEPPERS

Cavatelli means 'little hollows', but I also like to think of this dish as 'porcospino' (porcupine) pasta! It's easy and wonderful, handmade with a bit of love, and inspired by the spicy pasta Nonna Teresa made for me.

SERVES 4 | 1 HOUR 25 MINUTES

400g durum wheat flour or fine semolina flour, plus extra for dusting

olive oil

1 dried red chilli

1 dried red pepper (see page 226) or 1 teaspoon sweet paprika

½ a bunch of fresh thyme (15g)

1 large quality spicy sausage (125g)

1 red onion

2 cloves of garlic

125ml southen Italian white wine

1 x 400g tin of quality plum tomatoes

40g pecorino or Parmesan cheese

Pile the flour on to a clean surface and make a well in the middle. Gradually add 200ml of warm water, using a fork to bring the flour in from the outside until it forms a dough. Knead on a flour-dusted surface for 10 minutes, or until smooth and elastic. Cut the dough into four so you can work with it a quarter at a time. Cover the rest with a clean damp tea towel while you work, to stop it drying out. Roll your first quarter into a long sausage shape about 1cm in diameter, then cut it into 2cm chunks. Lightly flour the back of a fine grater, gently squash a chunk of dough against it with your thumb, then roll it off to create a nubbly, textured shape. Place on a semolina-dusted tray and repeat – you'll get the knack.

Place a large frying pan on a medium heat with 3 tablespoons of oil. Remove the stalks and seeds from the chilli and pepper, tear into flakes and add to the pan. Strip in the thyme leaves and fry for 30 seconds, or until crisp, then spoon out and save for later, leaving the pan on the heat. Squeeze the sausagemeat out of the skin into the pan and mash it up. Peel, finely chop and add the onion and garlic (and the paprika, if using), then fry gently for 15 minutes, or until soft, stirring occasionally. Add the wine, cook away, then mash in the tomatoes. Season and simmer for 15 minutes.

Cook the pasta in a pan of boiling salted water for 4 minutes, or until tender, then drain, reserving a mugful of starchy cooking water. Toss with the sauce, finely grate over most of the pecorino and toss again, loosening with a splash of reserved cooking water, if needed. Sprinkle over the chilli pepper mix and finely grate over the remaining pecorino, to finish.

CALORIES	FAT	SAT FAT	PROTEIN	CARBS	SUGAR	SALT	FIBRE
599kcal	19.4g	5.6g	19.7g	86.7g	6.3g	1.2g	4.5g

TUNA FETTUCCINE

BABY COURGETTES, CHERRY TOMATOES, PECORINO & CRUSHED ALMONDS

Cooking with Maria, the only fisherwoman on the island of Procida, just a stone's throw from Naples, inspired this dish. I love the way she uses pecorino as a seasoning, which is contrary to the 'no cheese and fish' rule, while the crushed almonds give texture, creaminess and depth of flavour. To make this recipe sing like Pavarotti, you really need baby or crunchy courgettes, so it's best made in the summer.

SERVES 4 | 20 MINUTES

50g whole almonds

1 small onion

2 cloves of garlic

4 anchovy fillets in oil

olive oil

300g dried fettuccine
  or linguine

4 baby courgettes,
  with flowers

300g yellowfin tuna

1 x 400g tin of quality
  cherry tomatoes

1 lemon

30g pecorino cheese

extra virgin olive oil

Lightly toast the almonds in a large frying pan on a medium heat, then tip into a pestle and mortar, leaving the pan on the heat. Peel the onion and garlic, finely chop with the anchovies and add to the pan with 2 tablespoons of olive oil. Fry for 4 minutes, stirring regularly.

Meanwhile, cook the pasta in a pan of boiling salted water according to the packet instructions. Slice the courgettes ½cm thick, reserving the flowers, chop the tuna into rough 1cm dice, then stir both into the frying pan. Scrunch in the tomatoes through your clean hands, squeeze over the lemon juice and leave to tick away, stirring regularly. Finely grate the pecorino. Pound the almonds until fine.

Once cooked, use tongs to drag the pasta straight into the frying pan, letting some starchy cooking water go with it. Toss together, then turn the heat off, tear in the courgette flowers and toss in the pecorino and most of the almonds. Check the seasoning, loosen with an extra splash of cooking water, if needed, and serve, sprinkled with the remaining almonds, finished with a drizzle of extra virgin olive oil.

CALORIES	FAT	SAT FAT	PROTEIN	CARBS	SUGAR	SALT	FIBRE
581kcal	23.3g	4.5g	34g	62.9g	8.6g	0.8g	3.7g

CHESTNUT TAGLIATELLE

SMOKED PANCETTA, VIN SANTO, PARMESAN & GOOD OIL

~~~~~~

For me, chestnuts and Vin Santo are the flavours of Tuscany, and an amazing pairing in this simple, elegant, delicate pasta. Propped up by the smokiness of crispy pancetta and a little Parmesan and parsley, this is a joy.

SERVES 2 | 45 MINUTES WITH FRESH PASTA

¼ x Royal pasta dough (see page 370) or 150g dried tagliatelle

4 rashers of smoked pancetta

1 onion

40g vac-packed chestnuts

40ml Vin Santo

½ a bunch of fresh flat-leaf parsley (15g)

40g Parmesan cheese

cold-pressed new season's extra virgin olive oil

Dried pasta is fine here, but silky, freshly made pasta will elevate this dish to another level. Start by making your Royal pasta dough (see page 370). Roll out the dough to 2mm thick, then, with a knife or fine roller cutters, cut into ribbons about 6mm wide. You could do this using the tagliatelle cutter on your pasta machine. Or, if using dried pasta, simply put it into a pan of boiling salted water to cook according to the packet instructions.

Finely slice the pancetta, place in a cold non-stick frying pan and put it on a medium heat so the fat renders out, while you peel the onion, then very finely slice it with the chestnuts. Add them to the pan to cook for 5 minutes, or until the onion is soft but not coloured, stirring occasionally. Pour in the Vin Santo and leave to tick away until the pasta's ready.

If using fresh pasta, drop it into a pan of boiling salted water for just 2 minutes. Either way, once cooked, use tongs to drag the pasta straight into the frying pan, letting some starchy cooking water go with it. Tear in the parsley leaves and finely grate in most of the Parmesan. Toss well to emulsify the sauce until it's delicate and smooth, adding an extra splash of cooking water, if needed. Season to perfection, then serve right away with a good drizzle of oil and the remaining Parmesan grated over.

CALORIES	FAT	SAT FAT	PROTEIN	CARBS	SUGAR	SALT	FIBRE
600kcal	29.7g	9.3g	23.9g	57.2g	9.3g	0.7g	3.9g

SAUSAGE LINGUINE

BROCCOLETTI, CHILLI FLAKES, GARLIC, WHITE WINE & PECORINO

The philosophy that a little can go a long way is so important, just as this dish proves. Being able to buy small amounts of ingredients as you need them, like one sausage, is a great reason to shop at markets. Go on, do it!

SERVES 2 | 15 MINUTES

150g dried linguine

200g broccoletti or sprouting broccoli

olive oil

1 large quality sausage (125g)

1 clove of garlic

2 anchovy fillets in oil

1 pinch of dried red chilli flakes

100ml Frascati white wine

20g pecorino or Parmesan cheese

extra virgin olive oil

Cook the pasta in a pan of boiling salted water according to the packet instructions, then drain, reserving a mugful of starchy cooking water.

Meanwhile, trim the broccoletti (halving any thick stalks lengthways to make them more delicate to eat). Place a large frying pan on a medium heat with 1 tablespoon of olive oil. Squeeze the sausagemeat out of the skin into the pan, breaking it up with a wooden spoon. Once lightly golden, peel, roughly chop and add the garlic, followed by the anchovies, chilli flakes, broccoletti and wine. Leave to bubble away while the pasta cooks.

Toss the drained pasta into the sausage pan, then finely grate over the pecorino and drizzle with extra virgin olive oil. Toss again, loosening with a little reserved cooking water, if needed, to create a light, creamy sauce. Taste and season to perfection, then serve right away.

CALORIES	FAT	SAT FAT	PROTEIN	CARBS	SUGAR	SALT	FIBRE
647kcal	30.7g	9.3g	28.2g	60.6g	5.2g	1.8g	6.2g

THE ORECCHIETTE NONNAS

ITRIA VALLEY | PUGLIA

Graziella, Comazia, Vita and Cinzia are lifelong friends who make fresh pasta from scratch, every day, using minimal ingredients to achieve maximum flavour. They each have a veg patch at the back of their trulli houses, so they cook with the seasons, using their own freshly picked produce to make delicious dishes. Due to her age and experience, Graziella is known as the queen of orecchiette (and trust me, local competition is fierce). She and her friends certainly put me and Gennaro to task when we cooked with them. Make your own orecchiette using the recipes on the pages that follow.

ORECCHIETTE

'LITTLE EARS' PASTA

There are a few techniques to making these little buggers. It's one of my favourite pasta shapes, but weirdly tricky to master. I don't want that to put you off – I've seen both 5-year-olds and 100-year-olds rattling it out in Italy very easily! Approach it with a Zen-like mind and I promise you'll get into the rhythm soon enough.

SERVES 4 | 1 HOUR 30 MINUTES

400g durum wheat flour or fine semolina flour, plus extra for dusting

Pile the flour on to a clean surface and make a well in the middle. Gradually add 200ml of warm water, using a fork to bring the flour in from the outside until it forms a dough. Knead on a flour-dusted surface, switching between fast and slow kneading, for 10 minutes, or until smooth and firm. Cut the dough into four so you can work with it a quarter at a time. Cover the rest with a clean damp tea towel while you work, to stop it drying out. Roll your first quarter into a long sausage shape about 1cm in diameter, then cut it into 1cm nuggets. Keep your surface well dusted with flour.

Now, method number one: starting at the edge furthest away from you, drag a blunt eating knife towards you over a nugget of dough, so it curls round and over the knife. Gently pull the dough off the knife, push your thumb inside and turn it inside out. Repeat, and you'll get it after a while. Method number two requires you to stick your thumb into the centre of a nugget (roll it into a ball first if you want to be more precise), rotate your thumb around to create a round disc, then pick the disc up and hold it between your thumb and forefinger, pulling it gently over your forefinger to make a similarly effective little ear. Transfer to a floured tray as you go.

Whichever method you choose, repeat with the remaining pasta, shaping and perfecting as you go until all your little ears are done.

CALORIES	FAT	SAT FAT	PROTEIN	CARBS	SUGAR	SALT	FIBRE
349kcal	1.6g	0.2g	10.6g	77.9g	0.6g	0g	2.9g

AUBERGINE & BLACK CHICKPEA ORECCHIETTE

SERVES 4 | 30 MINUTES, PLUS SOAKING

Soak **150g of dried black or regular chickpeas** overnight, then drain and cook according to the packet instructions, until soft. Trim **1 aubergine** and **1 courgette** and chop into 2cm dice, then peel and finely slice **1 onion**. Cook the veg in a large frying pan on a medium-high heat with **1 tablespoon of olive oil** for 15 minutes, or until soft, stirring occasionally. Drain the chickpeas, reserving the liquor. Stir the chickpeas into the veg pan with the juice of **½ a lemon**, loosening with a good splash of reserved liquor. Cook over a low heat for 8 more minutes, then taste and season to perfection with sea salt and black pepper. Meanwhile, cook your **fresh orecchiette** (see page 128) in boiling salted water for 4 minutes (or cook **300g of dried orecchiette** according to the packet instructions). Scoop the pasta into the sauce and toss together, loosening with pasta cooking water, if needed, then tuck in.

TOMATO & BROAD BEAN ORECCHIETTE

SERVES 4 | 30 MINUTES

Peel and finely slice **1 onion** and place in a wide shallow pan on a medium heat with **1 tablespoon of olive oil**. Stir occasionally while you pod **375g of new season's broad beans** (they're very small and tender, but if you can only get larger beans, simply pinch the skins off), then add them to the pan and cook for 6 minutes. Chop **250g of ripe tomatoes** into rough 1cm dice, then add to the pan. Season with sea salt and black pepper, then pick and tear in the leaves from **½ a bunch of fresh basil (15g)**. Meanwhile, cook your **fresh orecchiette** (see page 128) in boiling salted water for 4 minutes (or cook **300g of dried orecchiette** according to the packet instructions). Scoop the pasta into the sauce and toss together, loosening with pasta cooking water, if needed. Finely grate over **20g of salted ricotta or pecorino cheese** and toss again, finishing with an extra grating of cheese, if you like.

CORTECCIA

HOT SMASHED BROCCOLI, PECORINO, GARLIC & ANCHOVY PESTO

Corteccia, meaning 'tree bark', is also known as cavatelli, which comes from an Italian word meaning 'little hollows'. It's a great hands-on one to make with kids, and each unique piece is gnarly, bumpy and perfect for catching sauce. Served with this hot pesto, I have to say it's one of my wife's all-time favourite pasta dishes.

SERVES 4 | 1 HOUR 30 MINUTES

400g durum wheat flour or fine semolina flour, plus extra for dusting

400g sprouting broccoli or cime di rapa

olive oil

2 cloves of garlic

4 anchovy fillets in oil

1 pinch of dried red chilli flakes

40g pecorino or Parmesan cheese, plus extra to serve

extra virgin olive oil

1 lemon

Pile the flour on to a clean surface and make a well in the middle. Gradually add 200ml of warm water, using a fork to bring the flour in from the outside until it forms a dough. Knead on a flour-dusted surface, switching between fast and slow kneading, for 10 minutes, or until smooth. Follow the instructions on page 135 to shape your corteccia.

Trim the broccoli, halving any larger stalks lengthways so they cook evenly. Put a pan on a medium-high heat with 2 tablespoons of olive oil, then peel, slice and add the garlic, followed by the anchovies and chilli flakes. A couple of minutes later, add the broccoli and a pinch of sea salt and black pepper, then a splash of water to break the frying. Cover and cook for 10 minutes, then remove the lid for another couple of minutes. Tip the broccoli mixture on to a large board and finely chop it. Finely grate over the cheese, drizzle over 2 tablespoons of extra virgin olive oil and a squeeze of lemon juice, then mix, taste and tweak to your liking.

Cook the pasta in a pan of boiling salted water for 4 minutes, or until al dente. Retaining a little cooking water to emulsify the sauce, drain the pasta, return to the pan, toss in the broccoli pesto, then taste again for balance. Finish with extra virgin olive oil and an extra grating of cheese.

CALORIES	FAT	SAT FAT	PROTEIN	CARBS	SUGAR	SALT	FIBRE
544kcal	18.8g	4.3g	17.7g	81.3g	2.8g	1.3g	6.6g

HOW TO SHAPE CORTECCIA

Break marble-sized pieces off the dough and roll them into small, thin sausage shapes. One at a time, lay your fingers on top, then press down and drag the pasta back towards you to curl and create your shape, gently flicking the pasta pieces off your fingers so you don't squash them.

LASAGNE

SLOW-COOKED FENNEL, SWEET LEEKS & CHEESES

Being really single-minded in our commitment to drag out all the sweet deliciousness from fennel and leeks, this lasagne is an absolute cracker. Made and layered up with love, it's a confident and classy centrepiece.

SERVES 8–10 | 2 HOURS 20 MINUTES, PLUS COOLING

4 large leeks

3 bulbs of fennel

6 cloves of garlic

50g unsalted butter

½ a bunch of fresh thyme (15g)

125ml Soave white wine

75g plain flour

1.5 litres whole milk

1 whole nutmeg, for grating

50g pecorino or Parmesan cheese

100g Taleggio cheese

½ x Royal pasta dough (see page 370) or 400g dried lasagne sheets

125g ball of mozzarella cheese

100g Gorgonzola cheese

olive oil

Trim and slice the leeks and fennel, then peel and finely chop the garlic. Melt the butter in a large pan over a medium heat, strip in most of the thyme leaves, then stir in the veg. Season, then fry for 15 minutes, stirring regularly. Pour in the wine, cover, and cook for 30 minutes, or until soft and sweet, stirring regularly and adding splashes of water, if needed.

Stir in the flour for a few minutes, then gradually add the milk, a splash at a time, stirring constantly. Simmer until thickened, stirring occasionally. Finely grate in half the nutmeg. Remove from the heat, finely grate in half the pecorino, tear in half the Taleggio, and stir well. Taste and season to perfection with sea salt and black pepper, if needed, and leave to cool.

Preheat the oven to 180°C. If making Royal pasta dough (see page 370), roll out your dough to 2mm thick and cut into sheets. To assemble, layer up the sauce and pasta sheets in a large baking dish, adding little bombs of mozzarella, Gorgonzola and the remaining Taleggio as you go, finishing with a final layer of sauce. Finely grate over the remaining pecorino and any other bits of cheese, then bake for 40 minutes, or until golden and bubbling. Pick the remaining thyme leaves, toss in a little oil, and scatter over for the last 5 minutes. Leave to stand for 15 minutes, then dig in.

CALORIES	FAT	SAT FAT	PROTEIN	CARBS	SUGAR	SALT	FIBRE
584kcal	34.2g	18g	25.8g	42g	13g	1.8g	1.4g

MAKING RAVIOLI

On a well-floured surface, roll out your dough to 1mm thick. Spoon heaped teaspoons of filling evenly down long 14cm-wide pasta sheets, slightly off centre. Brush the exposed pasta lightly with water and fold the sheets in half over the filling. Gently seal around the filling, pushing out the air, then cut into 7cm squares. Place them on a semolina-dusted tray as you go.

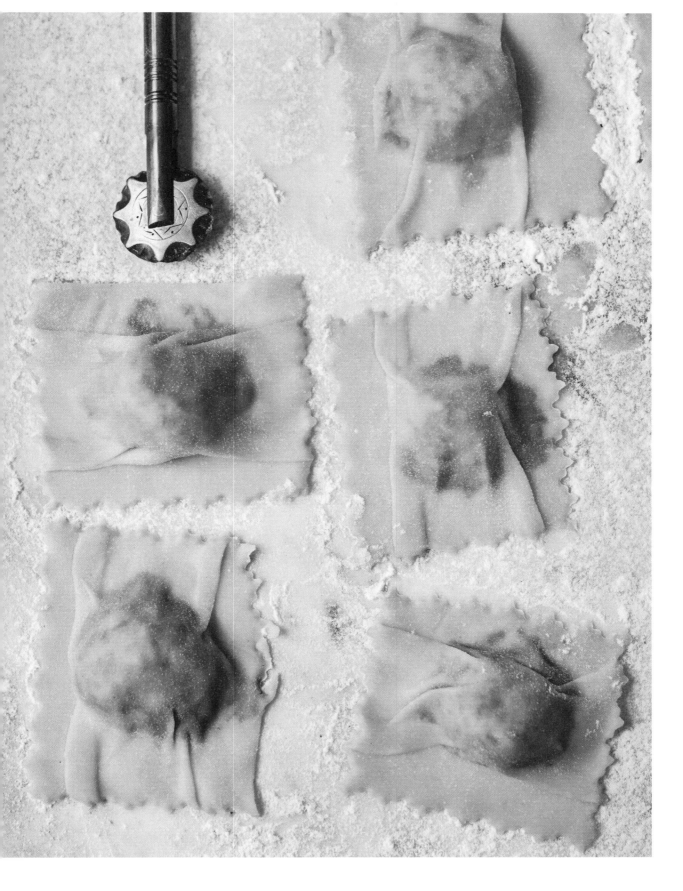

RAVIOLI

SEASONAL GREENS, MASHED POTATO & CHEESE

Perfecting the ritual of making ravioli is one of life's joys. It's not particularly hard but, like anything, practice makes perfect. My advice is to master the technique for yourself with time and patience, then unleash it on your dinner party. Delicate, thin pasta pillows filled with seasonal greens, mash, chilli and cheese – wow.

SERVES 6 | 2 HOURS, PLUS COOLING

¼ x Royal pasta dough
  (see page 370)

1 large potato (150g)

unsalted butter

1 clove of garlic

½–1 fresh red chilli

olive oil

150g mixed seasonal greens,
  such as wild garlic, chard,
  stinging nettles, spinach,
  rocket

40g pecorino or Parmesan
  cheese, plus extra to serve

1 whole nutmeg, for grating

1 lemon

Start by making your Royal pasta dough (see page 370). While it rests, peel and roughly chop the potato, then cook in a pan of boiling salted water for 15 minutes, or until tender. Drain, steam dry, then return to the pan and mash well with 2 knobs of butter and a pinch of sea salt and black pepper. Meanwhile, peel and finely slice the garlic, finely chop the chilli (deseed if you like), then fry in a non-stick frying pan on a medium heat with a splash of oil until lightly golden. Wash the greens, discarding any tough stalks. Saving a large handful of leaves for later, add the rest to the pan. Stir gently until wilted, then cook down until dark and all the excess moisture has cooked away. Turn the heat off and cool for 10 minutes.

To finish the filling, chop the greens super-finely and add to the mash. Finely grate over the pecorino and half the nutmeg, mix, taste and season to perfection. Follow the instructions on page 138 to make 24 ravioli.

Cook your ravioli 2 portions at a time in a pan of boiling salted water for just 2 minutes. Alongside, melt a large knob of butter in a frying pan on a medium-high heat, and fry 2 portions of your reserved raw green leaves until they crisp up nicely. Scoop the pasta straight on to two plates, pour over the butter and greens, shave over a little extra pecorino and finish with a good squeeze of lemon juice. Serve up to your first lucky guests, while you crack on with the next 2 portions. They'll love it.

CALORIES	FAT	SAT FAT	PROTEIN	CARBS	SUGAR	SALT	FIBRE
255kcal	17g	8.1g	7.3g	19g	1g	0.8g	1g

MAKING
AGNOLOTTI

On a well-floured surface, roll out your dough to
mm thick. I work with half at a time to give more
ontrol. Spoon heaped teaspoons of filling evenly
own long 8cm-wide pasta sheets. Brush the exposed
asta lightly with water and fold the sheets in half
ver the filling. Gently press each ball of filling
o flatten a little, seal around the filling, pushing
ut the air, then trim and fold the pasta again. Cut
etween the balls of filling to make little pillow
hapes, sealing and pinching the edges together,
lacing them on a semolina-dusted tray as you go.

ROASTED MEAT AGNOLOTTI

IN A SILKY PORCINI BROTH & BUTTER SAUCE

Agnolotti are iconic Piedmontese ravioli. Each piece of pasta is the perfect size and shape to savour as a heavenly mouthful, while the intensity and simplicity of the emulsified sauce give it a luxurious feel.

SERVES 8-10 | 3 HOURS

1 x Royal pasta dough
  (see page 370)

extra virgin olive oil

FILLING

1 onion

2 sticks of celery

2 cloves of garlic

4 rashers of smoked pancetta

olive oil

400g leftover cooked or
  roasted meat, such as
  chicken, pork, beef, game

2 sprigs of fresh rosemary

50g Parmesan cheese

1 whole nutmeg, for grating

SAUCE

750ml quality chicken stock

10g dried porcini mushrooms

75g unsalted butter

Start by making your Royal pasta dough (see page 370). While it rests, make the filling. Peel the onion, celery and garlic and finely chop with the pancetta. Place it all in a large frying pan on a medium-low heat with 1 tablespoon of olive oil. Cook for 10 minutes, or until soft but not coloured, stirring occasionally. For the sauce, pour the stock into a large pan, add the porcini and simmer over a medium heat until reduced by half.

Finely chop the leftover meat, add to the veg pan with the rosemary sprigs and cook very gently until the meat is soft. Pour in 100ml of the reduced stock and leave to cook away completely; you want the mixture to be quite dry. Remove the rosemary, finely grate in most of the Parmesan and a few scrapings of nutmeg, season to perfection, then leave to cool completely.

Follow the instructions on page 143 to make your agnolotti. In the large pan, reheat the remaining reduced stock over a medium-low heat, then whisk through the butter to make a silky sauce. Drop half the pasta into a large pan of boiling salted water for just 1 minute, then use a slotted spoon to scoop the pasta straight into the sauce. Cook the remaining pasta, then scoop that into the sauce, too. To serve, finely grate over the remaining Parmesan and drizzle each portion with a little extra virgin olive oil.

CALORIES	FAT	SAT FAT	PROTEIN	CARBS	SUGAR	SALT	FIBRE
629kcal	36.1g	12.1g	33g	43.8g	2.6g	0.5g	2.3g

RICE & DUMPLINGS

WHITE RISOTTO

THE MOTHER OF ALL RISOTTOS WITH BUTTER & PARMESAN

Simple and utterly delicious, this also stands as an immensely important recipe because it focuses on the art and ritual of cooking this starchy risotto rice to exactly the right, elegant consistency, then just flavouring it with quality butter and freshly grated Parmesan. If done correctly, it's pure luxury on a plate.

SERVES 4 | 45 MINUTES

1.2 litres quality chicken or
  veg stock

1 onion

2 sticks of celery

olive oil

2 knobs of unsalted butter

300g Arborio risotto rice

150ml Pinot Grigio white
  wine

60g Parmesan cheese

Simmer your chosen stock. Peel and finely chop the onion and celery, then place in a large, high-sided pan on a medium heat with 1 tablespoon of oil and 1 knob of butter (importantly, a high-sided pan gives more space and prevents the stock from evaporating too quickly, which can give an over-concentrated flavour). Cook for 10 minutes, or until softened but not coloured, stirring occasionally, then stir in the rice to toast for 2 minutes.

Pour in the wine and stir until absorbed. Add a ladleful of stock and wait until it's been fully absorbed before adding another, stirring for around 10 seconds every minute and continuing to add ladlefuls of stock until the rice is cooked. It will need 16 to 18 minutes. When I say cooked, I mean the rice is soft and a pleasure to eat, but importantly still retains its shape and a tiny bit of bite. At this point, add enough stock or water to give you a loose consistency. Beat in the remaining knob of butter, finely grate and beat in the Parmesan, then season to perfection and turn the heat off. Cover the pan and leave to relax for 2 minutes so the risotto becomes creamy and oozy. Beat again, then serve right away on warm plates.

CALORIES	FAT	SAT FAT	PROTEIN	CARBS	SUGAR	SALT	FIBRE
524kcal	18.9g	8.2g	18.4g	68.2g	3.7g	0.6g	2g

SAUSAGE & RED WINE RISOTTO

THYME, FENNEL, ONION, FONTINA & CRUSHED HAZELNUTS

Both comforting and luxurious, using a decent, drinking Barolo in this beautiful ruby risotto not only adds a lovely pink hue, but boldly brings the sweetness of the veg and the salty savouriness of the sausage together. With Parmesan, bombs of fontina and crunchy hazelnuts in the mix, it's an undeniably satisfying bowlful.

SERVES 4 | 45 MINUTES

1.2 litres quality chicken or veg stock

40g whole hazelnuts

1 red onion

½ a bulb of fennel

olive oil

2 knobs of unsalted butter

½ a bunch of fresh thyme (15g)

2 large quality sausages (125g each)

300g Arborio risotto rice

250ml Barolo red wine

50g Parmesan cheese

50g fontina cheese

extra virgin olive oil

Simmer your chosen stock. Put a large, high-sided pan on a medium heat and toast the hazelnuts as it heats up. Meanwhile, peel the onion, trim the fennel and finely chop both. Tip the hazelnuts into a pestle and mortar, returning the pan to the heat. Add 1 tablespoon of olive oil and 1 knob of butter, followed by the chopped veg, then strip in the thyme leaves (reserving the soft tips for garnish). Squeeze the sausagemeat out of the skins into the pan, breaking it up with the back of a wooden spoon. Cook for 10 minutes, stirring occasionally, then stir in the rice to toast. After 2 minutes, pour in the wine and stir until absorbed.

Now start adding the stock, a ladleful at a time, letting each one cook away before adding more, and stirring constantly for 16 to 18 minutes, or until the rice is cooked but still retains its shape. When done, add a splash of stock or water to make it oozy, then finely grate over most of the Parmesan, beat it in with the remaining butter, taste, and season to perfection. Turn the heat off, then bomb in little nuggets of fontina, so they melt subtly into the rice. Cover, and leave to rest off the heat for 2 minutes while you crush the nuts. Divide the risotto between warm plates, then finely grate over the remaining Parmesan. Sprinkle over the crushed nuts and thyme tips, then drizzle with extra virgin olive oil.

CALORIES	FAT	SAT FAT	PROTEIN	CARBS	SUGAR	SALT	FIBRE
839kcal	43.8g	17.1g	34.5g	70.6g	4.5g	1.8g	3.1g

OOZY BLACK RICE

SWEET ROASTED PEARS, THYME & CREAMY GORGONZOLA

It may not look traditionally Italian but believe me, Italians are growing, cooking and enjoying black rice just like this. It does take a bit longer to cook the rice to perfection, but it needs less hands-on attention than a regular risotto and is so worth it. I learnt this from a mondina nonna – it's super-comforting and a real joy.

SERVES 4 | 1 HOUR 30 MINUTES

2 litres quality chicken or
  veg stock

1 onion

2 sticks of celery

olive oil

300g black rice

150ml Barbera d'Asti red wine

4 firm pears

½ a bunch of fresh thyme
  (15g)

1 knob of unsalted butter

50g Parmesan cheese

100g Gorgonzola cheese

extra virgin olive oil

Preheat the oven to 180°C. Simmer your chosen stock. Peel and finely chop the onion and celery, then place in a large casserole pan on a medium heat with 1 tablespoon of olive oil. Cook for 10 minutes, or until soft but not coloured, stirring occasionally.

Stir the rice into the veg to toast for 2 minutes, then pour in the wine. Let it cook away, then pour in the stock, cover, and simmer for 1 hour, or until the rice is cooked, stirring occasionally and adding splashes of water, if needed. Meanwhile, peel, quarter and core the pears. In a baking dish, toss with a little olive oil, a pinch of sea salt and the thyme sprigs. Roast for 40 minutes, or until soft and golden.

To serve, beat the butter through the rice, then finely grate and beat in the Parmesan. Taste and correct the seasoning, if needed, then pour on to a serving platter. Top with the roasted pears, bomb over nuggets of Gorgonzola, and drizzle with a little extra virgin olive oil.

CALORIES	FAT	SAT FAT	PROTEIN	CARBS	SUGAR	SALT	FIBRE
488kcal	23.6g	11.3g	26.6g	35.2g	18.6g	1.6g	7.1g

NONNA ROSA

PO VALLEY | PIEDMONT

Nonna Rosa, like many of the other incredibly friendly folk I met at the rice fields, was in her youth what's known as a 'mondina', a seasonal rice worker, in the paddies of the Po River valley. What's wonderful is that all the nonnas still get together now, to cook traditional recipes and teach them to younger generations, like Alice and Simone who have left their city lives behind to move to the countryside and become rice farmers. The nonnas reminisce about their rice-picking days by singing old folk songs. Cooking with them was a joy – they're full of energy and high spirits, and their food is delicious.

PANISSA RICE

SMOKED PANCETTA, CURED MEATS, BORLOTTI BEANS, TOMATOES & RED WINE

Panissa is risotto's frumpy but very, very tasty cousin. The way the difference was explained to me by Rosa, who taught me, is that there's simply more in panissa so it's considered more of a whole meal than risotto is. You know it's ready when it's thick enough for your spoon to stand up in the middle – how cool is that.

SERVES 4 | 55 MINUTES

50g piece of smoked pancetta

50g salami

2 onions

2 sticks of celery

1 litre quality meat stock

1 bunch of fresh rosemary (30g)

300g Arborio risotto rice

250ml Barbera d'Asti red wine

1 x 400g tin of quality plum tomatoes

1 x 400g tin of borlotti beans

4 sprigs of fresh flat-leaf parsley

Chop the pancetta and salami into 1cm chunks, place in a cold casserole pan and put it on a medium-high heat to let the fat render out. Stir occasionally while you peel the onions and celery, then chop both into 1cm chunks. Stir the veg into the pan and cook for 10 minutes, or until soft, stirring regularly. In a separate pan, simmer the stock and rosemary.

Stir the rice into the veg to toast for 2 minutes, then pour in the wine and let it cook away. Scrunch in the tomatoes through your clean hands, then start adding the stock, a ladleful at a time, letting each one cook away before adding more. Keep a close eye on it and stir constantly for 20 minutes, or until the rice is cooked but still retains its shape. Drain the beans and stir into the pan with the last ladleful of stock. When your spoon stands up, it's done. Taste, and season to perfection with black pepper. Finely chop and stir in the parsley leaves, then tuck on in.

CALORIES	FAT	SAT FAT	PROTEIN	CARBS	SUGAR	SALT	FIBRE
545kcal	11.3g	3.9g	22.4g	82.6g	9.4g	1.4g	8.5g

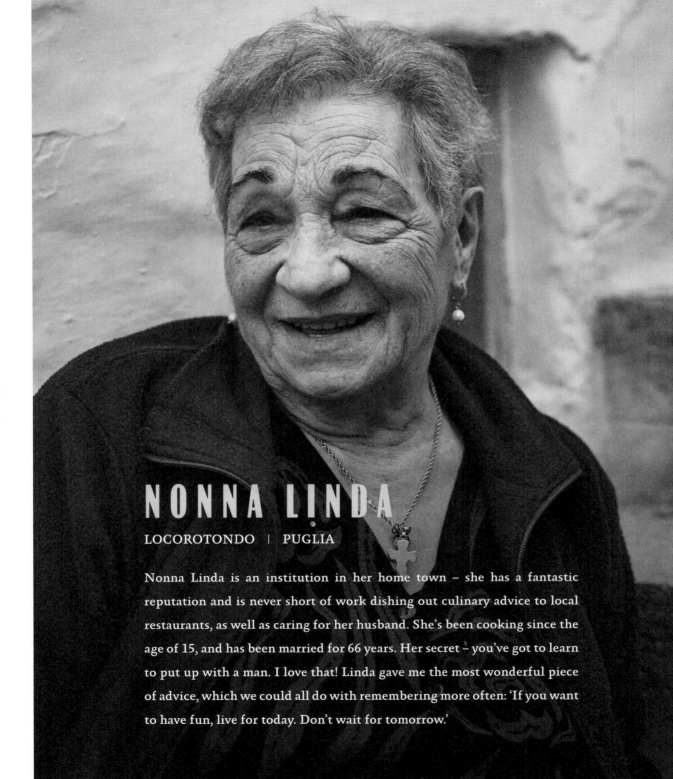

NONNA LINDA

LOCOROTONDO | PUGLIA

Nonna Linda is an institution in her home town – she has a fantastic reputation and is never short of work dishing out culinary advice to local restaurants, as well as caring for her husband. She's been cooking since the age of 15, and has been married for 66 years. Her secret – you've got to learn to put up with a man. I love that! Linda gave me the most wonderful piece of advice, which we could all do with remembering more often: 'If you want to have fun, live for today. Don't wait for tomorrow.'

BAKED TIELLA RICE

MUSSELS, COURGETTE, CHERRY TOMATOES, WHITE WINE & PARMESAN

The wonderful Nonna Linda and I laughed so much we cried when we cooked this dish, and to be honest, I've never seen anything like it before. It's a principle that can bow or step up to whatever budget you have. The genius thing is you simply prep all the veg so it cooks in the same time as the rice, meaning you can embrace different seasonal produce, which Linda was very cool about, ducking and diving so the recipe suits you.

SERVES 8 | 1 HOUR 30 MINUTES

300g potatoes

1 onion

1 clove of garlic

2 sticks of celery

400g ripe cherry tomatoes

1 bunch of fresh flat-leaf
   parsley (30g)

60g Parmesan cheese

400ml Prosecco

extra virgin olive oil

500g long-grain rice

750g mussels, scrubbed,
   debearded

1 courgette

Preheat the oven to 200°C. Peel the potatoes, then, one at a time, cut them lengthways into quarters and erratically slice them to about the thickness of a coin, the rougher the better. Place in an ovenproof earthenware pot or small casserole pan. Peel the onion, garlic and celery, then randomly finely chop with the tomatoes and parsley (stalks and all), and add to the pot. Finely grate in half the Parmesan, then pour in the Prosecco and 8 tablespoons of oil. Add the rice, season with sea salt and black pepper, then mix everything together really well.

Pick through the mussels and tap any open ones – if they don't close, discard. Now you've got two choices. Linda shucks the raw mussels, which is fiddly but you'll get the hang of it and it gives the most incredible depth of flavour from the sea. Use a small sharp knife to carefully prise open the shells and pull out each raw mussel and its juices. Or, simply put the mussels into a really hot pan, cover, and steam for 3 to 4 minutes until they pop open. Once cool enough to handle, remove the shells (discarding any that remain closed). Either way, stir the mussels and any juices into the pot, then finely slice the courgette and layer on top like a lid. Gently push down to submerge in the flavours, then finely grate over the remaining Parmesan. Place on a high heat, and as soon as it starts to bubble, transfer to the oven for 45 minutes, or until golden. Rest for 10 minutes, then serve.

CALORIES	FAT	SAT FAT	PROTEIN	CARBS	SUGAR	SALT	FIBRE
472kcal	16g	3.4g	13.2g	65g	4.2g	0.7g	2.6g

BAKED RISOTTO PIE

SWEET SPICY SQUASH & OOZY CHEESES

A crispy baked risotto pie is a thing of beauty, especially when stuffed with nutty spiced squash and gorgeous oozy cheeses. This dish can be served as an antipasto, or an aperitivo, but it also makes a wonderful lunch or dinner. Simply pair it up with a fresh rocket salad and a nice glass of wine – what's not to love?

SERVES 8-10 | 1 HOUR 30 MINUTES, PLUS COOLING

1 x White risotto
  (see page 148)

400g butternut squash

2 cloves of garlic

1 fresh red chilli

olive oil

1 sprig of fresh rosemary

100g fine stale breadcrumbs

75g mixed melty cheeses, such
  as fontina, Parmesan,
  Cheddar

125g ball of mozzarella cheese

2 lemons

Make the White risotto (see page 148) the night before you need it, but don't loosen it with extra stock, just add butter and Parmesan, so your risotto is firm enough to hold its shape. Cool it quickly and keep in the fridge overnight. The next day, deseed the squash and chop into 1cm cubes, peel and roughly chop the garlic, and finely slice half the chilli. Place it all in a large frying pan on a medium heat with 2 tablespoons of oil and the rosemary sprig. Season lightly with sea salt and cook for 8 minutes, or until just starting to soften, stirring regularly. Now, stir in the risotto.

Preheat the oven to 200°C. Scrunch up a sheet of wet greaseproof paper, then flatten it out and rub generously with oil. Scatter over half the breadcrumbs, then use the sheet to line a deep baking tray (20cm x 30cm), crumb side up. Spoon in two-thirds of the risotto, discarding the rosemary. Flatten the risotto along the base and up the sides to create a receptacle for the cheese. Roughly chop and scatter in the melty cheeses, tear over the mozzarella, then spoon over the remaining risotto, smoothing the top. Sprinkle with the remaining breadcrumbs, then bake at the bottom of the oven for 1 hour, or until golden and crisp. Leave to stand for 10 minutes, then use the paper to lift out on to a board, and slice. Finely chop and scatter over the remaining chilli and serve with lemon wedges, for squeezing over. It's a wonderfully oozy, crumbly, delicious plateful.

CALORIES	FAT	SAT FAT	PROTEIN	CARBS	SUGAR	SALT	FIBRE
417kcal	19.1g	8.5g	16.4g	44.9g	4.5g	1g	2g

NONNA MERCEDES

GRESSONEY-ST-JEAN | AOSTA VALLEY

Wonderful Nonna Mercedes is one of the few remaining direct descendants of the Walsers, a community with both Swiss ancestry and Germanic roots that chose to settle in Italy. She lives high in the mountains, and continues to cook traditional Walser recipes, such as the chnéffléné – semolina teardrop dumplings – you see on the pages that follow. It's such a unique and fun recipe, and I've shared a few different sauces, so please give it a go.

SEMOLINA TEARDROP DUMPLINGS

AKA CHNÉFFLÉNÉ BY NONNA MERCEDES

When Nonna Mercedes taught me this recipe, my first thought was what a brilliant way to cook. Using simple ingredients, it really represents the survival cooking typical of the Walser community. It's delicate, delicious, cheap and quick to put together, and has already become a firm favourite of mine. It reminds me of Alpine gnocchi and you can treat it like pasta. Essentially it's batter that drips into boiling water to cook into tender teardrop dumplings ready to be tossed with something wonderful.

SERVES 4 | 45 MINUTES, PLUS RESTING

3 large eggs

300ml whole milk, plus extra for loosening

200g Tipo 00 flour

200g fine semolina flour

1 whole nutmeg, for grating

Whisk the eggs and milk together in a large bowl. Gradually whisk in the Tipo 00 flour, followed by the semolina flour, a pinch of sea salt and black pepper, and a good few crude scrapings of nutmeg to form a fairly thick but still totally pliable and gloopy batter. Leave to rest for 30 minutes.

Half-fill a large pan with salted water and bring up to a fast rolling boil. In the mountains they have a special gadget to pass the batter through, but to make this accessible I use a regular metal colander with ½cm holes, which you need to hold under cold running water before use (this helps prevent the batter from sticking to it. I also recommend loosening the batter with extra milk, if needed, just before you cook it, so it is just loose and gloopy enough to almost reluctantly cry through the holes into the water, where it immediately sets into firm, beautifully peculiar dumplings).

Working quickly, pour half the batter into the colander and use a clean hand or a large metal whisk to swirl and push it around, encouraging it to fall through the holes of the colander, straight into the water. The teardrop dumplings will cook in just 2 or 3 minutes, so once done, sieve out into your chosen sauce (see pages 168 to 171), and cook the second batch.

CALORIES	FAT	SAT FAT	PROTEIN	CARBS	SUGAR	SALT	FIBRE
453kcal	9.1g	3.3g	20.1g	75.9g	4.1g	0.8g	2.3g

NONNA MERCEDES' FONDUTA

SERVES 4 | 10 MINUTES

Grate **150g of fontina cheese** into a heatproof bowl with a splash of **whole milk**. Separate **1 large egg**, adding the yolk to the bowl (save the white for another recipe). Sit the bowl over a pan of very gently simmering water, making sure the water doesn't touch the base of the bowl, and leave to slowly melt for 4 to 5 minutes, until silky, almost like a thick custard. Whisk regularly, loosening with more milk, if needed, then season well with black pepper and a few scrapings of **nutmeg**. Toss with your **dumplings** (see page 166) and a splash of their cooking water to loosen, if needed.

ROASTED RED ONION & BACON

SERVES 4 | 1 HOUR 15 MINUTES

In a tray, roast **4 unpeeled red onions** in the oven at full whack (240°C) for 1 hour, or until burnt on the outside and soft. Chop **4 rashers of smoked streaky bacon** 1cm thick and place in a large cold frying pan. Put on a medium heat so the fat renders out. Squeeze the sweet onions out of their skins and chop, adding to the pan when the bacon sizzles. Strip in the leaves from **2 sprigs of fresh rosemary**. Cook and stir for 5 minutes. Toss with your **dumplings** (see page 166) and a splash of their cooking water to loosen. Finish with a little **extra virgin olive oil** and a fine grating of **Parmesan cheese**.

PESTO & RICOTTA

SERVES 4 | 10 MINUTES

Think of this one as more of a principle. I want to show you just how wonderfully versatile this delicate little dumpling recipe is – you can basically use any of my pesto recipes on page 377, or the cavalo nero pesto from my Polenta gnocchi on page 180. Spoon **4 tablespoons of your chosen pesto** into a frying pan on a low heat, stirring to warm through for a few minutes. Toss with your **dumplings** (see page 166) and a splash of their cooking water to loosen, if needed. Finely grate over some **salted ricotta or a little pecorino cheese**, then finish with a little drizzle of **extra virgin olive oil**.

GARLIC MUSHROOM

SERVES 4 | 20 MINUTES

Peel and finely chop **1 onion** and **2 cloves of garlic**, then place in a large frying pan on a medium heat with **1 tablespoon of olive oil** and **1 knob of unsalted butter**. Cook for 5 minutes, or until softened, stirring regularly. Tear in **300g of wild mushrooms** and cook for another 5 minutes, continuing to stir regularly. Toss with your **dumplings** (see page 166) and a splash of their cooking water to loosen. Finely grate in **40g of Parmesan cheese** and toss or stir over the heat to emulsify the sauce. Taste and season to perfection, then finish with a little **extra virgin olive oil** and an extra grating of Parmesan.

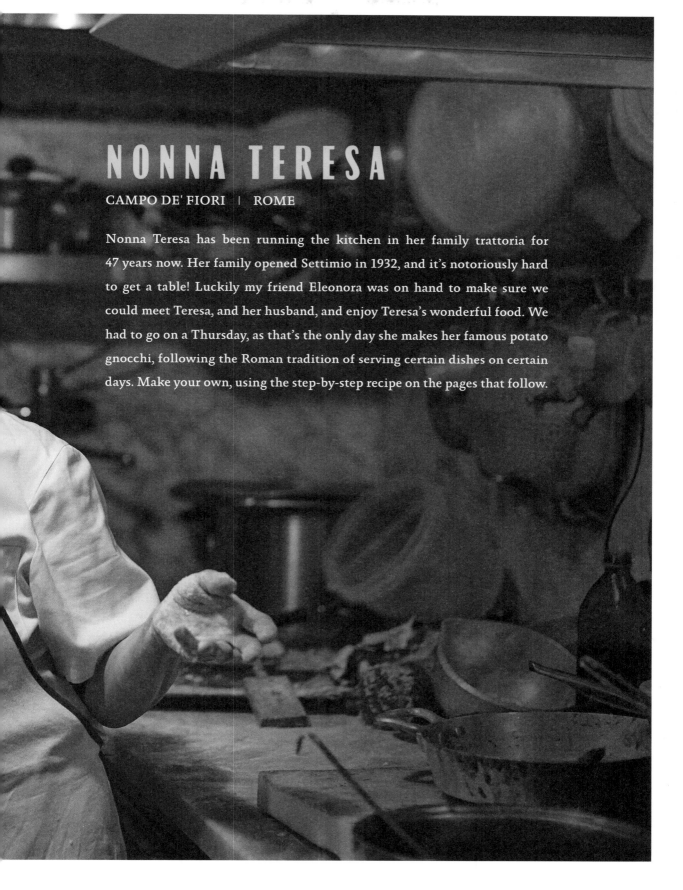

NONNA TERESA

CAMPO DE' FIORI | ROME

Nonna Teresa has been running the kitchen in her family trattoria for 47 years now. Her family opened Settimio in 1932, and it's notoriously hard to get a table! Luckily my friend Eleonora was on hand to make sure we could meet Teresa, and her husband, and enjoy Teresa's wonderful food. We had to go on a Thursday, as that's the only day she makes her famous potato gnocchi, following the Roman tradition of serving certain dishes on certain days. Make your own, using the step-by-step recipe on the pages that follow.

POTATO GNOCCHI

LIGHT, FLUFFY PILLOWS OF JOY

~~~~~~

In Rome, Nonna Teresa introduced me to this method, which doesn't use eggs. For restaurant service, when the gnocchi mix is made in advance, eggs are useful, but cooked this fresh you don't need them. She believes the fresher the mix, the lighter the gnocchi, and she's right – you get a very good result with this recipe. It's an amazing gift to be able to make good gnocchi at home. It's quick to cook, very cheap, and total comfort food.

SERVES 6–8 | 1 HOUR 30 MINUTES

1kg floury potatoes, such as Maris Piper, King Edward

100g Tipo 00 flour, plus extra for dusting

1 whole nutmeg, for grating

Use potatoes of a fairly even size, as you're going to cook them whole. Cook in a large pan of boiling salted water for 20 to 25 minutes, or until tender. Drain and leave until cool enough to handle, then remove the skins. Mash the potatoes using a potato ricer or masher on to a large clean board. Sprinkle over the flour, finely grate over half the nutmeg, season well with sea salt and black pepper, then scrunch and push the mixture together with clean hands. Depending on the potatoes, you may need to add a little more flour – use your common sense.

Knead on a flour-dusted surface for a few minutes until pliable, then divide into 4 equal pieces and roll each into a sausage about 2cm thick. Slice into 3cm lengths – this is your basic gnocchi. Now you can gently roll each piece down a butter pat, the back of a fork or a fine grater to add grooves, which will help your sauce to stick, or simply roll into balls.

Nonna Teresa cooked her gnocchi 2 portions at a time, as it's so quick, and it also means they're less likely to break up. Cook in a pan of boiling salted water for 2 to 3 minutes – as soon as they come up to the surface they're ready. Remove with a slotted spoon and toss with melted butter and finely grated Parmesan, my Hero tomato sauce (see page 372), or leftover sauce from a stew (try the Mixed meat ragù on page 228, which you can see in the picture), then finely grate over a little Parmesan, to serve.

CALORIES	FAT	SAT FAT	PROTEIN	CARBS	SUGAR	SALT	FIBRE
181kcal	0.6g	0.1g	5.7g	40.1g	1.3g	0.4g	2.7g

SEMOLINA GNOCCHI

ROMAN-STYLE WITH SMOKY PANCETTA, GARLICKY TOMATOES & OOZY TALEGGIO CHEESE

This is a fun dish to make. It's essentially a thick semolina porridge, poured out and set to give you discs that you then cook over sweet tomato sauce. The pancetta and Taleggio add extra oomph on the flavour front.

SERVES 4 | 50 MINUTES, PLUS SETTING

1 litre semi-skimmed milk

1 knob of unsalted butter

1 whole nutmeg, for grating

250g fine semolina

2 large eggs

50g Parmesan cheese, plus extra for baking

olive oil

1kg ripe cherry tomatoes

75g piece of smoked pancetta

1 clove of garlic

1 pinch of dried red chilli flakes

100g Taleggio cheese

Pour the milk into a pan on a medium heat and bring to a simmer, then stir in the butter and a good grating of nutmeg. Whisking constantly, gradually pour in the semolina, whisking until thickened. Turn the heat off, whisk in just the egg yolks (save the whites for another recipe), finely grate and mix in the Parmesan, then pour into a large oil-rubbed roasting tray and spread into an even layer. Refrigerate for 1 hour, or until set.

Meanwhile, preheat the oven to 200°C. Prick each tomato with the tip of a sharp knife, blanch in a pan of boiling salted water for 40 seconds, then drain. Once cool enough to handle, pinch off the skins. Finely slice the pancetta and place in a cold shallow ovenproof pan. Place on a medium heat so the fat renders out while you peel, finely chop and add the garlic, along with the chilli flakes and 2 tablespoons of oil. Once lightly golden, add the peeled tomatoes, and season well with sea salt and black pepper. Transfer to the oven to roast for 15 minutes, then remove.

Turn the tray of set semolina out on to a board, then stamp out discs with a 5cm round cutter (bake the offcuts with oil and herbs for a chef's treat). Layer the discs over the tomatoes, then poke in little pieces of Taleggio. Season from a height, finely grate over a fine layer of Parmesan, then bake for 20 to 25 minutes, or until golden and bubbling. For extra colour, whack the pan under the grill for a few minutes before serving.

CALORIES	FAT	SAT FAT	PROTEIN	CARBS	SUGAR	SALT	FIBRE
707kcal	35.7g	16.1g	33g	68.8g	19.5g	3.3g	3.9g

POLENTA GNOCCHI

CAVOLO NERO PESTO & PARMESAN

This polenta gnocchi is a bit of a revelation, and a recipe that Gennaro just loves to make. You can toss it with any sauce, though this super-quick green pesto is delicious with it. You'll love the flavour and cute shape.

SERVES 6 | 45 MINUTES, PLUS SETTING

250g coarse polenta

olive oil

1 clove of garlic

200g cavolo nero or kale

50g Parmesan cheese, plus extra to serve

30g pine nuts

cold-pressed extra virgin olive oil

To make the polenta, simply follow the packet instructions, seasoning generously. Coarse polenta takes around 40 minutes, while the finer one can be ready in as little as 10 minutes – you can buy it pre-made, which is convenient, but I prefer to make it. When it comes easily away from the sides of the pan, it's good to go. Tip into an oiled baking tray (20cm x 30cm), press into an even layer, cool, and refrigerate for 1 to 2 hours, or until set. Tip out on to your work surface and cut into bite-sized nuggets.

For the pesto, peel the garlic and plop into a large pan of boiling salted water. Tear out and discard the cavolo nero stalks, adding the leaves to the pan. Blanch for 4 minutes, then use a slotted spoon to scoop the garlic and cavolo into a blender, leaving the water on a high heat. Finely grate the Parmesan into the blender, add the pine nuts and 6 tablespoons of extra virgin olive oil, then whiz until super-smooth. Season to perfection, loosening with water, if needed, then tip into a large frying pan.

Drop half the gnocchi into the rapidly boiling salted water for just 2 minutes, then transfer to the pesto pan with a slotted spoon, and repeat. Toss the gnocchi and pesto together over the heat, loosening with cooking water. Finish with a drizzle of extra virgin olive oil and more Parmesan.

CALORIES	FAT	SAT FAT	PROTEIN	CARBS	SUGAR	SALT	FIBRE
329kcal	18g	3.5g	7.2g	34g	0.9g	0.3g	2.4g

GNUDI

RICOTTA, HERO TOMATO SAUCE & SPROUTING BROCCOLI

Delicate gnudi – meaning 'naked' – is basically a ravioli without the pasta. To have success, you need to hunt out really good ricotta, but boy, are the results worth it – this is comfort personified. You can even gratinate it, taking things to a whole new gnudi dimension. Alternatively, serve simply with sage butter and Parmesan.

SERVES 6-8 | 1 HOUR 30 MINUTES, PLUS CHILLING

1kg quality crumbly ricotta

100g Parmesan cheese, plus
  extra to serve

1kg fine semolina, for dusting

1 x Hero tomato sauce
  (see page 372)

200g sprouting broccoli or
  cime di rapa

unsalted butter

1 whole nutmeg, for grating

Drain the ricotta and place in a bowl with a pinch of sea salt and black pepper, then finely grate in the Parmesan. Beat together, then taste and perfect the seasoning. Cover a large tray with the semolina, then shape the ricotta mixture into 4cm balls, rolling them in the tray of semolina as you go until really well coated. You should get 48 gnudi in total. Sprinkle, shake and cover them all really well with the semolina, then leave for at least 8 hours in the fridge, turning halfway (don't cover the tray). The semolina coating will dehydrate the ricotta, also forming an outer layer.

Make your Hero tomato sauce (see page 372) and keep it warm. Trim the broccoli stalks and finely slice the spears lengthways to make them more delicate to eat. The gnudi will only take 3 minutes to cook and I like to cook them 2 portions at a time so they don't bash into each other. So, shake the excess semolina off 2 portions of gnudi and cook them in boiling salted water with 2 portions of the broccoli. Spoon some tomato sauce into two warmed serving bowls. Scoop the gnudi and broccoli into a separate bowl, and add a knob of butter and a fine grating of nutmeg. Toss gently to coat, then spoon on to the sauce and finish with an extra grating of Parmesan. Serve up while you crack on with the next 2 portions.

Or, to make things easy for a dinner party, pour the sauce into a baking dish, sit all the cooked, dressed gnudi and broccoli on top, finely grate over some Parmesan and place under a hot grill until golden and bubbling.

CALORIES	FAT	SAT FAT	PROTEIN	CARBS	SUGAR	SALT	FIBRE
569kcal	31.8g	17.4g	30g	43.8g	10.4g	1.2g	3.8g

MEAT

CHICKEN BASTARDO

GARLIC, BAY, CHILLIES & VINEGAR

Welcome to chicken bastardo, baby! Look, you will probably think the amount of garlic, bay and chillies here is outrageous, but because everything is left whole as it cooks you get a big but wonderfully gentle, round, warm, delicious flavour, and the vinegar mingles with that beautifully. You don't actually have to eat the chillies if you don't want to, you could simply peel, deseed and put them under oil for use another day.

SERVES 6 | 1 HOUR 30 MINUTES

1 x 2kg whole chicken

olive oil

20 cloves of garlic

20 fresh bay leaves

20 fresh mixed-colour chillies

100ml red wine vinegar

optional: 1 tablespoon
   runny honey

Preheat the oven to 180°C. Put a large ovenproof frying pan on a high heat. Joint the chicken (see page 386), placing the pieces in the pan skin side down as you go, along with 2 tablespoons of oil. Fry for 15 minutes, turning regularly until all the pieces are lovely and golden all over.

Make some space in the pan, then add the whole unpeeled garlic cloves and the bay leaves. Prick and add the chillies. Fry for 2 minutes, mix everything together, then pour in the vinegar, add a splash of water and season well. Cover with a scrunched-up sheet of wet greaseproof paper and place in the oven for 45 to 50 minutes, or until golden and cooked through. Sometimes I drizzle over honey when it comes out of the oven.

To serve, divide up the chicken between your plates. Peel the chillies, scrape out the seeds, then chop the flesh and, to taste, stir it back through the pan juices. Squeeze the sweet garlic out of its skins into the pan, stir together, then spoon as much as you like over the chicken. Delicious with a simple side salad and a loaf of good bread. Sometimes I serve the chicken on a platter, then toss freshly cooked spaghetti through the pan juices to enjoy on the side – a very delicious option.

CALORIES	FAT	SAT FAT	PROTEIN	CARBS	SUGAR	SALT	FIBRE
386kcal	21.4g	5.3g	41.1g	6.4g	2.4g	0.3g	0.7g

FIORENTINA STEAK

CRISPY BEEF FAT POTATOES & SALSA VERDE

Bistecca alla Fiorentina is the king of all Italian steaks. It's essentially a fat T-bone or porterhouse steak, which is normally cooked quite blue. It's delicious, but I prefer it cooked medium-rare. I think it's important to cook one big steak, which means you can look after it better and build up more flavour and colour on the outside, leaving you with the most delicious, blushing, juicy inside. Traditionally, Fiorentina steak is cooked over hot coals, but I've written this to be cooked in a pan so it's more accessible. With crispy potatoes and salsa verde to complement it, this is an amazing treat-night dinner for four lucky people.

SERVES 4 | 1 HOUR 10 MINUTES

1kg T-bone steak, 5cm thick

1kg red-skinned potatoes

1 bulb of garlic

3 sprigs of fresh rosemary

SALSA VERDE

1 bunch of fresh mint (30g)

1 bunch of fresh flat-leaf
  parsley (30g)

1 bunch of fresh basil (30g)

2 tablespoons capers in brine

2 gherkins

2 anchovy fillets in oil

2 tablespoons red wine
  vinegar

2 teaspoons Dijon mustard

extra virgin olive oil

Get your steak up to room temperature before you cook it. Wash the potatoes and cut into 3cm chunks. Parboil in a pan of boiling salted water with the whole unpeeled garlic cloves for 8 minutes. Meanwhile, trim the fat on the steak to 1cm thick and put the steak aside. Finely chop the fat offcuts, place in a large cold frying pan and put on a medium-high heat to render the fat. Once sizzling, drain and add the potatoes and garlic. Cook for 30 minutes, or until golden and crisp, stirring occasionally. Strip in the rosemary leaves for the last 2 minutes, then leave on the lowest heat.

Meanwhile, put a separate cold, non-stick frying pan on a medium-high heat and use tongs to hold the steak fat edge down for 6 minutes to render the fat and get it dark golden. Turn on to the bone edge for another 6 minutes to heat the bone. Now, gently turn the steak on to one of its flat sides. Cook for 6 minutes on each flat side (or 8 minutes for medium-rare). Remove to a board, cover, and rest, pouring pan juices over the potatoes.

Pick the mint, parsley and basil leaves into a food processor. Pulse, then add the rest of the salsa verde ingredients with 8 tablespoons of oil. Blitz to your desired consistency, then taste and season to perfection. I like to carve and season the steak at the table, serving it with the crispy spuds and salsa verde alongside. Squeeze the sweet garlic out of its skins and enjoy.

CALORIES	FAT	SAT FAT	PROTEIN	CARBS	SUGAR	SALT	FIBRE
695kcal	43.2g	10.7g	30.6g	46.2g	2.2g	0.9g	3.9g

STUFFED BRAISED CELERY

SAUSAGE, MINCED MEAT, BREAD & HERBS IN A CHERRY TOMATO & WINE RAGÙ

It's so nice to celebrate celery – an often forgotten and underrated veg – as the centre-stage hero of this dish. Here, it's the most amazing edible shell for the tasty, meaty stuffing. Trust me, you're going to love this one.

SERVES 4-8 | 2 HOURS 20 MINUTES

150g sourdough bread

2 quality sausages (150g total)

200g minced veal or pork

2 teaspoons dried oregano, thyme or rosemary

1 whole nutmeg, for grating

olive oil

2 large heads of celery

2 onions

4 cloves of garlic

150ml Gavi di Gavi white wine

2 x 400g tins of quality cherry tomatoes

Preheat the oven to 180°C. Tear the bread into a bowl and pour over 400ml of water. Squeeze the sausagemeat out of the skins into a separate bowl, add the mince, dried herbs and a pinch of black pepper, then finely grate in half the nutmeg. Squeeze the excess water out of the bread, add it to the mix with 2 tablespoons of oil, then scrunch together.

Reserving any yellow leaves, trim the ends of the celery stalks, so you're left with two heads about 20cm in length. Wash well, then use a speed-peeler to remove the base and stringy outer edges. Holding the base of one head in the palm of your hand and trying to keep the head in one piece, ease the stalks apart and start stuffing in half the mince mixture, pushing it right down between the stalks and sticking them together as you go. When it's compact, hold it together by securing with string. Repeat with the second head and the remaining mince. Place them in a high-sided roasting tray (25cm x 30cm). Cover with tin foil and roast for 1 hour.

Meanwhile, peel and finely slice the onions and garlic. Place in a large non-stick frying pan on a medium heat with 1 tablespoon of oil and cook for 5 minutes, stirring regularly. Pour in the wine and let it cook away, then add the tomatoes and 2 tins' worth of water. Leave to simmer on the lowest heat, stirring occasionally, until the time's up on the celery. Pour the sauce into the tray, then return to the oven, uncovered, for 40 minutes, turning the heads halfway. To serve, halve or quarter each head lengthways, spoon over the sauce and sprinkle with any reserved leaves.

CALORIES	FAT	SAT FAT	PROTEIN	CARBS	SUGAR	SALT	FIBRE
464kcal	23.4g	6.4g	24.4g	34.8g	12.8g	1.5g	5.4g

PORK SHOULDER

TENDER & SLOW-ROASTED WITH LOTS OF BAY, GARLIC, ONIONS & VINEGAR

~~~~~~

Cooking this illustrious cut of pork should be reserved for a great occasion, party or feast. It's probably some of the easiest cooking you'll ever do – simply source a wonderful piece of quality pork from your butcher and let the oven do all the hard work. I've developed this method over many years, using a high temperature at the start to create epic crackling, then cooking slow at a lower temp to give you melt-in-the-mouth tender meat.

SERVES 20 | 8 HOURS, PLUS RESTING

6 red onions

2 bulbs of garlic

20 fresh bay leaves

1 whole pork shoulder,
  bone in (5–7kg)

olive oil

200ml red wine vinegar

Preheat the oven to full whack (240°C). Place the whole onions and garlic bulbs in a large, deep-sided roasting tray with the bay. Use a clean Stanley knife to carefully score the pork skin all over at 1cm intervals (or ask your butcher to do this for you). Drizzle and rub all over with oil, then sprinkle with sea salt and rub it in well. Sit the pork in the tray, skin side up. Roast for 40 minutes to 1 hour, or until the skin is crisp.

Pour the vinegar around the pork, then reduce the oven to 130°C and cook for 7 hours. I don't baste this cut, as the natural distribution of fat is wonderful, but it is worth adding 250ml of water to the tray after about 2 hours, then checking it every hour or so after that to make sure that the base doesn't dry out or burn, keeping the meat nice and juicy.

When the time's up, the crackling should be super-crisp and the meat beneath should easily pull apart. Carefully lift the meat on to a board to rest. Skim all the fat from the tray into a jam jar for cooking with another day. Squeeze the onions and garlic out of their skins back into the tray and stir in 400ml of boiling water to create a simple and flavoursome saucy dressing, by scraping up the sticky bits with a wooden spoon.

To serve, pull off the crackling, then shred the meat apart with two forks and pour over the dressing. Brilliant as part of a roast dinner, in sandwiches or as part of a buffet. Leftovers are great in a stuffed pasta.

CALORIES	FAT	SAT FAT	PROTEIN	CARBS	SUGAR	SALT	FIBRE
381kcal	28.1g	8.8g	26.8g	5.1g	3.1g	0.3g	1.1g

NONNA ROSINA

LITTLE LUCANIAN DOLOMITES | BASILICATA

Back in the day, Nonna Rosina was a shepherd herself, and she still likes to get out to walk with the sheep when her health allows. Her son, Domenico, has taken over, and is the fifth generation of the family to do so. Sadly, he is one of only four remaining shepherds on the mountainside, where there used to be hundreds. The family can never leave their sheep unattended, as local wolves are regular predators. Because of their surroundings, they've honed their mountainside cooking to perfection. We enjoyed a lovely pastorale – or lamb stew – with the family, and I was inspired to give you a classic Stuffed leg of lamb recipe in their honour on the pages that follow.

STUFFED LEG OF LAMB

MINT, ANCHOVIES, BREAD, GARLIC & CAPERS

This is a wonderful way to flavour and enjoy a leg of lamb. In the pictures you'll see I cooked two the old-fashioned way over fire, and of course you're welcome to do the same if you can, but I've written this recipe for roasting in a standard oven. Get some lovely local lamb from your butcher and get them to bone it, too.

SERVES 8-10 | 1 HOUR 45 MINUTES

150g stale rustic bread

50ml Prosecco

olive oil

1 lemon

4 cloves of garlic

1 dried red chilli

1 bunch of fresh mint (30g)

4 anchovy fillets in oil

1 tablespoon baby capers
  in brine

1 large butterflied leg of
  lamb, boned but shank
  bone left in (2.5kg)

Preheat the oven to 200°C. Tear the bread into rough 2cm chunks and place in a food processor, then pour over the Prosecco, drizzle with 1 tablespoon of oil, finely grate in the lemon zest and squeeze in the juice. Season generously with sea salt and black pepper, then leave to soak for 10 minutes. Peel the garlic and roughly chop with the chilli, pick the mint leaves, and add to the processor with the anchovies and capers. Pulse into crumbs, then taste and season to perfection, if needed.

Lay the lamb leg on a board, skin side down. Massage all over with a pinch of salt and pepper, then spoon over the stuffing in an even layer. Roll up the leg meat to seal the filling inside, then tie at regular intervals with six lengths of string to make sure the stuffing is secure. Place straight on to the bars of the oven, with a tray underneath to catch the juices. Roast for 1 hour 10 minutes, or until the lamb is golden, yet still blushing and pink in the middle (cook for a further 10 to 15 minutes if you prefer your lamb well done). Rest for 5 minutes, while you simmer the tray of drippings on a medium heat with a little water, stirring to pick up any nice sticky bits. Slice the lamb and spoon over the tray juices. Beautiful served with roast potatoes and seasonal veg – or I love it stuffed into a sandwich.

CALORIES	FAT	SAT FAT	PROTEIN	CARBS	SUGAR	SALT	FIBRE
292kcal	14.4g	4.7g	30.2g	10g	0.6g	1.2g	0.4g

CHICKEN SKEWERS

WRAPPED IN PROSCIUTTO WITH SALSA VERDE STUFFING, POTATOES & TOMATOES

This is such fun – we cook wrapped, stuffed chicken thighs across two skewers so they get crisp and gnarly on the outside, then we slice between them to reveal the tender white meat inside. The potatoes are the real star – they suck up the chicken juices as they cook, becoming wonderfully stodgy and melt-in-your-mouth.

SERVES 6 | 1 HOUR 20 MINUTES

60g blanched almonds

6 cloves of garlic

1 tablespoon balsamic vinegar

1 tablespoon baby capers
  in brine

6 anchovy fillets in oil

1 bunch of fresh flat-leaf
  parsley (30g)

10 skinless, boneless chicken
  thighs

10 slices of prosciutto

1.2kg potatoes

300g ripe cherry tomatoes

olive oil

1 bunch of fresh thyme (30g)

extra virgin olive oil

Preheat the oven to 200°C. Put the almonds into a food processor and pulse to rough crumbs. Peel and add the garlic, add the balsamic and capers, the anchovies and a splash of their oil, then tear in the top leafy half of the parsley and pulse until fairly fine. Open the chicken thighs out on to a board, smooth side down, and pound with your fist or a rolling pin until flattened and tenderized. Divide the stuffing between them and roll up, wrapping each thigh in a slice of prosciutto. Double skewer 5 thighs across two long metal skewers, then repeat.

Peel the potatoes and slice 1cm thick, then parboil in a large pan of boiling salted water for 6 minutes. Prick each tomato with the tip of a sharp knife and add to the pan for the last 40 seconds, then drain it all. Once cool enough to handle, pinch the skins off the tomatoes. Layer the potatoes in a large, sturdy baking dish, seasoning with sea salt and black pepper, and drizzling lightly with olive oil as you go, then scatter over the tomatoes. Nestle the skewers on top so that all the tasty juices drip down over the potatoes as they cook. Roast for 30 minutes. Dip the bunch of thyme in olive oil, then use it as a brush to baste the chicken and potatoes with the pan juices. Sprinkle the thyme sprigs over the dish and return to the oven for a final glorious 10 minutes. Slice between the skewers, then drizzle with extra virgin olive oil, to serve. If you like your potatoes super-crisp, pop them back into the oven for an extra 10 minutes at the end.

CALORIES	FAT	SAT FAT	PROTEIN	CARBS	SUGAR	SALT	FIBRE
479kcal	20.3g	4.2g	37g	39.5g	4.2g	1.9g	3.5g

SAUSAGE, BEANS & GREENS

SPIKED WITH GARLIC, SWEET ONION, ANCHOVIES & ROSEMARY

Three hero ingredients, cooked with love and precision, make for a joyful meal. This recipe relies on you using great-quality ingredients, and I like to cook in a relaxed manner, slowly braising the greens, crisping up the sausages and beautifully redressing the beans. Enjoyed with a glass of Chianti on the side, it's heaven.

SERVES 4 | 30 MINUTES

1 red onion

4 cloves of garlic

2 anchovy fillets in oil

olive oil

4 large quality sausages
  (125g each)

4 sprigs of fresh rosemary

640g mixed seasonal greens,
  such as cime di rapa,
  tenderstem broccoli, cavolo
  nero, kale, dandelions

red wine vinegar

1 x 700g jar of white beans

extra virgin olive oil

Peel and finely slice the onion and garlic and place in a large, deep frying pan on a medium heat with the anchovies and a splash of olive oil. Fry until soft and lightly golden, stirring regularly. Place the sausages in a separate snug-fitting pan with a little oil on a medium-low heat to cook through and crisp up for about 20 minutes, turning occasionally. With 5 minutes to go, strip the rosemary leaves into the sausage juices to crisp up.

Meanwhile, wash the greens, removing any tough stalks and halving any thick broccoli stalks lengthways to make them more delicate to eat, then toss into the onions (in batches, if needed). Add a splash of water, cover, and braise for 10 to 15 minutes, or until dark and tender. Taste, and season to perfection with sea salt, black pepper and about 1 tablespoon of vinegar.

Remove the cooked sausages to a warm plate. Pour the beans into the empty pan (juice and all), turn the heat up, boil, and season to perfection with salt, pepper, a little vinegar and a drizzle of good extra virgin olive oil. Divide the beans between your plates, place a gnarly sausage alongside, and finish with the braised greens.

CALORIES	FAT	SAT FAT	PROTEIN	CARBS	SUGAR	SALT	FIBRE
574kcal	36.1g	11.9g	38.1g	21.1g	6.2g	2.4g	11.7g

CHICKEN UNDER A BRICK

PAN-ROASTED & DROWNED IN SALSA PICCANTE SALUBRE

By cooking under a brick (al mattone) you speed up the cooking process – we preheat the bricks so the chicken cooks from both sides. Also, the weight tenderizes and creates increased surface area for the skin to get wonderfully crispy – genius. This chicken is naked when cooked, then fully submerged in the salsa to rest, where it sucks up all the incredible flavours. Any leftover salsa can then be stored for future use.

SERVES 6 | 1 HOUR 30 MINUTES

1 red onion

3 cloves of garlic

3 fresh red chillies

1 tablespoon fennel seeds

1 bunch of fresh mint (30g)

1 bunch of fresh flat-leaf
  parsley (30g)

300ml extra virgin olive oil

100ml red wine vinegar

1 x 2kg whole chicken

olive oil

Preheat the oven to full whack (240°C). Get yourself two bricks, wash them well, then completely cover each with a triple layer of tin foil. Place in the oven with a large pan or roasting tray to heat through.

Meanwhile, to make the salsa, peel the onion and garlic, then finely chop with the chillies and place in a bowl with the fennel seeds. Rip off the top leafy half of the mint and parsley, including any tender stalks, then finely chop and add to the bowl with the extra virgin olive oil and vinegar. Add 1 teaspoon each of sea salt and black pepper, and mix well.

Use a large sharp knife to carefully cut the chicken in half lengthways. Slash the thighs and drumsticks at 3cm intervals and rub all over with a little olive oil. Carefully remove the pan and bricks from the oven, then place the chicken in the pan, skin side down. Place a hot brick on each chicken half, press down, then cook in the oven for 45 minutes, or until golden and cooked through. Remove the bricks and pour the salsa straight over the chicken halves in the pan, ensuring they're well covered. Leave to rest for 10 minutes, then pull the chicken out of the salsa on to a platter and serve. I like to place any leftover salsa in the fridge for up to 3 days, or freeze it – it's delicious for cooking with any meat, fish or veg.

CALORIES	FAT	SAT FAT	PROTEIN	CARBS	SUGAR	SALT	FIBRE
458kcal	36.2g	7g	31.4g	1.5g	1g	0.6g	0.3g

ITALIAN HAM, EGG & CHIPS

PANELLE CHICKPEA CHIPS & POT-ROAST ROSEMARY PORK

~~~~~~

This dish is so much fun and the panelle chips – crispy on the outside, soft in the middle – are just delicious. They're usually served as an antipasto with cured meats, cheese and pickles, or alongside drinks at aperitivo hour, but I've chosen to celebrate them as part of one of my favourite childhood dishes – ham, egg and chips.

SERVES 8 | 1 HOUR 40 MINUTES

olive oil

450g gram flour

1kg skinless, boneless pork loin

1 bunch of fresh rosemary (30g)

4 tablespoons white wine vinegar

8 large eggs

Grease a roasting tray (25cm x 35cm) with oil. Pour 1.6 litres of water into a large pan. Whisking constantly, add the gram flour, then place the pan on a high heat and bring to the boil, continuing to whisk the mixture until nice and thick – this will take about 8 minutes. Season to perfection with sea salt and black pepper, then, working quickly before the batter sets, pour it into the oiled tray and spread into an even layer. Leave to cool slightly, then pop into the fridge for 1 hour, or until set.

Meanwhile, preheat the oven to 180°C. Score the pork fat in a criss-cross fashion, rub with a little oil, then place in a snug-fitting casserole pan on a high heat, for about 8 minutes, turning with tongs until brown all over. Stir the rosemary bunch into the pan, season the pork with salt and pepper, then roast for 40 minutes, or until tender and cooked through. Remove from the oven and pour in the vinegar, moving the pork around until the vinegar sizzles, then cover and leave to rest.

Flip the set batter out on to an oiled board and cut lengthways into three long strips, then across into 2cm-thick chips. Toss them in oil to coat, then roast in a single layer in two baking trays for 45 minutes, or until crispy, turning halfway. Just before they're done, finely slice the pork and toss with its resting juices, and fry the eggs to your liking. Plate up the dressed pork, crispy chips and fried eggs, drizzle over any extra juices, and tuck in.

CALORIES	FAT	SAT FAT	PROTEIN	CARBS	SUGAR	SALT	FIBRE
676kcal	45.9g	13.8g	39.5g	28.4g	1.5g	0.6g	6g

POT-ROAST RABBIT

SWEET PEPPERS, SMOKED PANCETTA, GARLIC, WINE & ROSEMARY

This truly spectacular dish is a joy to make. Get your butcher to order you in a rabbit – wild or farmed – and joint it for you. Keep the offal – the flavour it adds is what gives this dish its traditional taste. I also make this recipe with pheasant, partridge or chicken, or even a mixture, all of which give delicious results.

SERVES 4 | 1 HOUR 15 MINUTES

50g piece of smoked pancetta

1 whole rabbit (1.2kg),
  skinned, jointed, with offal

olive oil

75g unsalted butter

2 red peppers

2 yellow peppers

1 bulb of garlic

½ a bunch of fresh rosemary
  (15g)

2 anchovy fillets in oil

300ml Soave white wine

white wine vinegar

Preheat the oven to 190°C. Chop the pancetta into 2cm lardons. Generously season the rabbit meat and offal from a height with sea salt and black pepper, drizzle with 1 tablespoon of oil, and toss to coat.

Melt 50g of butter in a large, sturdy, ovenproof pan on a medium heat. Add all the rabbit except the offal, and cook for 5 minutes, or until golden, turning regularly while you deseed the peppers and tear them into thumb-sized chunks. When the rabbit is golden, pour away the melted butter, and add the remaining fresh butter to the pan. Stir in the pancetta and the offal (it adds such depth and deliciousness, but if offal isn't your thing, simply finely chop it first so you still get the flavour, but won't even notice it's in there). Break apart the garlic bulb, tossing the unpeeled cloves straight into the pan with the rosemary sprigs and anchovies. Keep everything moving, and when it has good colour, stir in the peppers. Pour in the wine and let it reduce by half.

Cover the rabbit with a scrunched-up sheet of wet greaseproof paper, then transfer to the oven for 40 minutes, basting halfway. Remove the paper, add a splash of vinegar to cut through the sweetness, and cook for a further 10 minutes, or until the meat is beautifully tender. Great served with rice, chunks of bread, a simple salad or sautéed diced potatoes.

CALORIES	FAT	SAT FAT	PROTEIN	CARBS	SUGAR	SALT	FIBRE
564kcal	33.2g	15.6g	44.4g	10.2g	7.6g	1.5g	4g

NONNA ELENA

PITIGLIANO | TUSCANY

What a gentle, inspirational woman Nonna Elena is. The last Jewish nonna in Pitigliano, a town that used to be known as 'little Jerusalem' because of its Jewish community, Elena has lived through a lot of history, surviving the Second World War by hiding out in caves near the town to avoid persecution. Elena's recipe is an old family favourite, but she finds it too tiring to cook any more, so she wanted me to take that baton and pass it on to you. You'll find Jewish artichokes on the pages that follow.

JEWISH ARTICHOKES

STUFFED WITH MEAT & HERBS, FRIED & BRAISED IN TOMATO SAUCE

I really want to keep this recipe from Nonna Elena, the last Jewish nonna in Pitigliano, alive. It can be enjoyed as an antipasto or secondo, or even served with pasta. I've stayed true to the method she shared with me, including an interesting backwards tomato sauce – you boil tomatoes and drop in raw veg to cook!

SERVES 4–8 | 2 HOURS 30 MINUTES

2 x 400g tins of quality plum tomatoes

1 onion

1 clove of garlic

1 stick of celery

½ a bunch of fresh basil (15g)

½ a bunch of fresh flat-leaf parsley (15g)

6 Italian violet artichokes

2 lemons, for artichoke prep

200g plain flour

4 large eggs

400g lean minced beef

1 pinch of dried red chilli flakes

vegetable oil, for frying

Put a casserole pan that will snugly fit the artichokes later on a medium-high heat. Scrunch in the tomatoes through your clean hands, then pour in 2 tins' worth of water. Peel and finely chop the onion, garlic and celery. Finely chop half the basil leaves and half the parsley (stalks and all). Stir it all into the pan, simmer for 30 minutes to thicken and reduce the sauce, then taste and season to perfection.

Meanwhile, prep the artichokes (see page 382), then quarter each one lengthways, dropping the pieces back into the lemon water. Put the flour into a shallow bowl, and beat 2 eggs in another shallow bowl. Place the mince in a bowl with the chilli flakes and a good pinch of sea salt, and crack in the remaining 2 eggs. Finely chop the remaining basil leaves and parsley, add to the bowl, then scrunch and mix together, and divide into eight. Take one piece, then press and hug 3 artichoke quarters together around it, packing and squeezing it back into its original shape. Roll it in the flour, dunk it in the beaten egg, letting any excess drip off, then pop on a tray ready to fry. Repeat until you have 8 re-formed artichokes.

Meanwhile, pour 5cm of vegetable oil into a large, sturdy, deep-sided pan on a high heat. Get it to 160°C on a thermometer, then gently lower all 8 artichokes into the oil – they'll pack it out. Fry for 10 minutes, or until golden, then use a slotted spoon to lift them into the sauce. Reduce to a medium-low heat, simmer for 10 minutes, turning halfway, then serve.

CALORIES	FAT	SAT FAT	PROTEIN	CARBS	SUGAR	SALT	FIBRE
686kcal	37.7g	8.5g	38.9g	53g	12.4g	1g	4.1g

WILDEST BOAR RAGÙ

SPRINKLED WITH PARSLEY, GARLIC & LEMON GREMOLATA

This is a homage to Nonna Miriam's style of cooking, letting time and heat do all the work – cooking low and slow creates incredible depth and tenderness. Feel free to bolster your base with other seasonal root veg.

SERVES 10-12 | 5 HOURS, PLUS MARINATING OVERNIGHT

1 x 3kg wild boar, pork or lamb shoulder, bone in, skin removed

4 tablespoons juniper berries

4 fresh bay leaves

4 tablespoons wine vinegar

olive oil

2 bulbs of fennel

4 red onions

4 carrots

750ml Chianti red wine

100g tomato purée

1 bunch of fresh rosemary (30g)

GREMOLATA

1 bunch of fresh flat-leaf parsley (30g)

1 clove of garlic

1 lemon

The night before you want to cook, marinate the boar in a large tray. Smash up the juniper berries in a pestle and mortar and rub over the meat with the bay, vinegar and 4 tablespoons of oil. Cover and refrigerate.

The next day, put your largest casserole pan on a medium-high heat. Trim and roughly chop the fennel (reserving any leafy tops in a bowl of cold water), and place in the pan with 2 tablespoons of oil. Peel and roughly chop the onions and carrots, stir in with a good pinch of sea salt, then cook for 15 to 20 minutes, or until softened and golden, stirring occasionally.

Meanwhile, wipe any excess marinade off the meat, then sear in a large frying pan on a high heat, turning with tongs until browned all over. Sit the meat in the veg pan, pour over the red wine, stir in the tomato purée, add another pinch of salt, then just cover everything with water. Tie up and submerge the rosemary. Bring to a simmer, cover, and cook for 4 to 5 hours, or until tender, turning the meat and stirring the veg occasionally. Gently pull the meat apart, removing the bones and sinew, stir back through the sauce, then loosen to your desired consistency with water.

For the gremolata, pick the parsley leaves, then finely chop with the reserved drained fennel tops. Crush over the garlic through a garlic crusher, finely grate over the lemon zest, then keep chopping and mixing until fine. Scatter over the hot ragù and serve right away with Oozy polenta (see page 368), creamy mashed potato, crusty bread or pasta.

CALORIES	FAT	SAT FAT	PROTEIN	CARBS	SUGAR	SALT	FIBRE
523kcal	29.7g	8.5g	38g	12.9g	9.4g	0.8g	4g

NONNA MIRIAM

PANZANO | TUSCANY

Nonna Miriam reminded me of the gifts of restraint and patience when it comes to cooking. She encouraged me to forget the cheffy techniques I've learnt over the years and go with my instincts, clanking stuff up however felt right. Miriam believes that the modern pace of life is too fast and, coupled with the accessibility of convenience food, leads people to believe they don't have time to cook. She wants us to celebrate and pass on traditional skills, recipes and knowledge, so that old flavours and classic combinations aren't lost for ever. Turn the page for her Stracotto recipe.

STRACOTTO

BEAUTIFUL SLOW-COOKED BEEF RAGÙ

A Tuscan family favourite: think the emotion of Bolognese on the familiarity scale, but with a whole new level of comfort. It's inspired by Nonna Miriam from Panzano, and this simple cooking process gives you what she calls a 'rich plate' – she likened it to the moment you know you've got a winning hand in poker. To serve, it's traditional to enjoy the rich sauce with freshly cooked tagliatelle as a primo, serving the rest of the sauce with the meat as a secondo, teamed with steamed greens, oozy polenta, mash or whatever you fancy!

SERVES 8 | 4 HOURS

1kg piece of beef chuck, sinew removed

olive oil

2 red onions

2 carrots

2 cloves of garlic

2 sticks of celery

1 bulb of fennel

½ a bunch of fresh rosemary (15g)

½ a bunch of fresh sage (15g)

250ml Chianti red wine

2 tablespoons tomato purée

1.5 litres quality meat or veg stock

Place the meat in a fairly snug-fitting casserole pan on a medium-low heat with 2 tablespoons of oil, turning with tongs, while you peel the onions, carrots and garlic, trim the celery and fennel, then roughly chop it all to make a soffritto – it cooks low and slow so there's no need to be too precise. Stir into the pan, tie the rosemary and sage together and add, then season with sea salt and black pepper. Cook for 20 to 30 minutes, or until starting to caramelize, stirring the veg and turning the meat occasionally.

Turn the heat up to high, pour in the wine, stir in the tomato purée, and let the wine cook away. Pour in the stock, bring to the boil, then place a double layer of scrunched-up wet greaseproof paper on the surface. Reduce to a low heat and cook for around 3 hours, or until the meat is meltingly tender, turning and basting occasionally. Season to perfection.

Lift the meat out on to a board, carve it into thin slices, and spoon over enough of that incredible sauce to keep the meat nice and juicy. Toss the rest of the sauce (reduce on the hob, if needed) with freshly cooked tagliatelle, and finely grate over a little Parmesan, to serve. Double win.

CALORIES	FAT	SAT FAT	PROTEIN	CARBS	SUGAR	SALT	FIBRE
360kcal	20.6g	7.2g	30.6g	8g	6.2g	0.7g	2.6g

STUFFED PEPPERS

SPICY 'NDUJA, FENNEL SEEDS, MINCED PORK, RICOTTA & OREGANO

These stuffed peppers are an absolute treat to eat. Cooking the peppers empty to start off with means you invest time in their natural flavour, creating the perfect foundation for all those wonderful fillings to sing. It's well worth hunting out 'nduja, a truly delicious Calabrian spiced meat that's packed with extra flavour.

SERVES 4 | 1 HOUR 10 MINUTES

2 large or 3 medium red
  peppers

olive oil

250g minced pork shoulder

1 tablespoon fennel seeds

20g 'nduja

50g coarse stale sourdough
  breadcrumbs

extra virgin olive oil

1 lemon

4 sprigs of fresh oregano

½ teaspoon dried red
  chilli flakes

250g quality crumbly
  ricotta cheese

Preheat the oven to 180°C. Halve the peppers lengthways and deseed. Sit them cut side up in a snug-fitting ovenproof pan or roasting tray. Drizzle with 1 tablespoon of olive oil, season from a height with sea salt and black pepper, then rub all over. Roast for 30 minutes.

Meanwhile, use your clean hands to scrunch the minced pork with the fennel seeds and a pinch of pepper until well mixed. Tear in the 'nduja, add the breadcrumbs, and loosely mix through the mince, giving you a marbled effect. Pour 2 tablespoons of extra virgin olive oil into a separate bowl. Finely grate in the lemon zest and squeeze in the juice. Strip in the oregano leaves, add the chilli flakes, season, and toss together.

When the time's up on the peppers, loosely divide the mince mixture between them, then crumble over the ricotta. Return to the oven for another 30 minutes, or until golden and delicious, sprinkling over the dressed herbs and any oil from their bowl for the last 5 minutes. Delicious served with a fresh, crunchy seasonal salad.

CALORIES	FAT	SAT FAT	PROTEIN	CARBS	SUGAR	SALT	FIBRE
334kcal	25g	7.7g	17.4g	11g	4.5g	1.5g	2.2g

BEEF CHEEK RAGÙ

BAROLO, TOMATOES, CINNAMON & CLOVES

Beef cheeks, when cooked gently, are one of the most delicious parts of the whole animal. Inspired by Nonna Miriam and her obsession for slow-cooking and making tough, cheaper cuts of meat the hero, this is amazing served with mashed potato, crusty bread or oozy polenta, or even tossed with freshly cooked pasta.

SERVES 10 | 4 HOURS 50 MINUTES

20g dried porcini mushrooms

5 beef cheeks, trimmed

olive oil

150g piece of smoked pancetta

½ a celery heart

2 red onions

2 carrots

5 cloves

8 cloves of garlic

½ a cinnamon stick

1 bunch of mixed fresh herbs (30g), such as sage, bay, rosemary, thyme, basil, parsley

500ml Barolo red wine

1 x 680g jar of passata

Preheat the oven to 160°C. Cover the porcini with boiling kettle water and leave to rehydrate. Season the beef cheeks with sea salt and black pepper, then brown them in a large casserole pan on a high heat with a splash of oil, turning until well coloured all over. Meanwhile, slice the pancetta into lardons. Peel the celery, onions and carrots, then chop into rough 1cm dice. In a pestle and mortar, crush the cloves with 1 teaspoon each of salt and pepper, then peel and pound in the fresh garlic.

When brown, push the cheeks to one side of the pan and reduce to a medium heat. Add the pancetta and cinnamon, stirring until the pancetta is lightly golden. Drain the porcini, reserving the liquor, then roughly chop and add to the pan with the veg. Tie the herbs together, then stir in with the garlic mixture. Fry for 15 minutes, or until soft, stirring occasionally.

Pour in the wine, let it reduce by half, then pour in the reserved porcini water (discarding just the last gritty bit) and the passata. Fill the passata bottle with water and pour into the pan. Cover with a scrunched-up sheet of wet greaseproof paper and a lid. Cook in the oven for 4 hours, or until the meat is outrageously tender and the sauce has thickened. Taste the sauce and season, if needed, then serve up however you wish.

CALORIES	FAT	SAT FAT	PROTEIN	CARBS	SUGAR	SALT	FIBRE
359kcal	12.6g	4.8g	19.6g	16.4g	11.6g	2.2g	3g

SALINA CHICKEN

BEAUTIFUL, SCENTED SOFT AUBERGINES & TOMATOES WITH CAPERS

Celebrating the flavours of the island of Salina, Nonna Marina inspired me to embrace the beautiful bounty growing in her back garden and create this dish, perfect for a feast. Sumptuous, comforting, melt-in-your-mouth chicken, gentle spice and delicious, buttery aubergines. With a glass of cold white wine, it's pure joy.

SERVES 6 | 2 HOURS

3 aubergines (750g total)

1 x 1.4kg whole chicken

olive oil

2 cloves of garlic

3 small fresh red chillies

1 cinnamon stick

4 sprigs of fresh woody herbs, such as rosemary, thyme, bay

50g baby capers in brine

2 red onions

200g ripe cherry tomatoes

50g pine nuts

2 lemons

4 sprigs of fresh basil

Trim the aubergines, chop into random 5cm chunks and wedges, place in a large bowl and season generously from a height with sea salt. Put aside.

Joint the chicken (see page 386). Drizzle all the pieces with oil, place in a large shallow pan on a medium-high heat, skin side down, to get golden on all sides, then remove to a large platter. Wipe the salt off the aubergines and add to the pan, turning until lightly golden on all sides. Remove the aubergines to the platter and reduce the heat under the pan to low. Peel and slice the garlic, prick the chillies and place both in the pan with the cinnamon, woody herbs and capers. Stir and fry for a couple of minutes while you peel and finely slice the onions, then stir them into the pan, too. Cook for 15 minutes, or until starting to caramelize, stirring occasionally.

Preheat the oven to 180°C. Squeeze the tomatoes in a bowl of water to remove the seeds – a fine nonna trick to prevent you getting splattered – then tear them into the pan. Put the chicken and aubergines back in, drizzle over any resting juices, then pour in 600ml of water. Sprinkle over the pine nuts, then squeeze over the lemon juice. Cook at the bottom of the oven for 45 minutes, or until golden. Pick over the basil leaves and serve with a nice big bowl of lemony couscous.

CALORIES	FAT	SAT FAT	PROTEIN	CARBS	SUGAR	SALT	FIBRE
299kcal	18.2g	3.7g	26.2g	8.3g	6.8g	1g	1g

ITALIAN LAMB KEBABS

BREAD, GARLICKY WILD HERB MARINADE & PECORINO PARSLEY MASH

~~~~~~

This is an incredible lamb kebab dish with thin slices of offal and smoky cured meat, beautifully marinated and skewered with bread and bay. In southern Italy they have mild, sweet, dried peppers that they toast in olive oil and shatter over dishes. They're hard to find, so here's a method for drying jarred peppers instead.

SERVES 8 | 1 HOUR 15 MINUTES, PLUS MARINATING OVERNIGHT & DEHYDRATING

1 leg of lamb, boned, sinew removed (1.2kg)

350g sourdough bread

200g lamb's liver, trimmed

2 lamb's kidneys, trimmed

100g piece of guanciale (cured pig's cheek) or smoked pancetta

24 fresh bay leaves

1 bunch of fresh oregano (30g)

2 cloves of garlic

75ml red wine vinegar

extra virgin olive oil

1 x 600g jar of peeled, roasted red peppers

1.2kg potatoes

75g pecorino cheese

½ a bunch of fresh flat-leaf parsley (15g)

Preheat the oven to 100°C. Slice the lamb into rough 3cm chunks, about 1cm thick. Slice the bread into pieces the same size. Finely slice the liver, kidneys and guanciale, which will act as subtle flavourings. Put it all into a large bowl with the bay. Strip the oregano leaves into a pestle and mortar. Peel the garlic and add with 1 teaspoon of sea salt and a good pinch of black pepper, then pound into a paste. Muddle in the vinegar and 4 tablespoons of oil, then toss with the meat and bread, cover, and marinate overnight. Drain the peppers, pat dry with kitchen paper, rub with a little oil, tear in half, then lay on a tray lined with greaseproof paper. Leave to dry out in the oven for 4 hours, then remove.

The next day, make up 8 skewers, be they metal, wood (soak in water first) or rosemary, interspersing the offal, guanciale and bay between the lamb and the bread. Peel the potatoes, halving any larger ones, then cook in a pan of boiling salted water for 20 minutes, or until tender. Meanwhile, cook the kebabs on the medium side of your barbecue, or in a griddle pan on a medium heat, for 15 minutes, turning until gnarly all over, but still blushing in the middle – you may need to work in batches. Drain the potatoes, steam dry, then return them to the pan and mash well. Finely grate over the cheese, finely chop and add the parsley leaves, mix in 6 tablespoons of oil and season to perfection. Divide up the mash, slice everything off the skewers and tear over the crispy peppers.

CALORIES	FAT	SAT FAT	PROTEIN	CARBS	SUGAR	SALT	FIBRE
801kcal	44.2g	14.5g	49.3g	52.3g	3.5g	2.2g	3.1g

MIXED MEAT RAGÙ

CHICKEN, SAUSAGE, RIBS, PORCINI, WINE & TOMATOES

~~~~~~

Inspired by my time with Nonna Teresa, this beautiful recipe gives you not only a delicious stew, but also a wonderful sauce that's perfect paired with Potato gnocchi (see page 176). A lot of Roman cooking originates in the old meat-market district of Testaccio, and makes the most of cheaper cuts, like ribs. Using a whole chicken, including the giblets, is a more economical way to shop, but also adds more flavour. Enjoy.

SERVES 12 | 3 HOURS 40 MINUTES

1 x 1.8kg whole chicken,
  with giblets

6 large quality sausages
  (125g each)

20g dried porcini mushrooms

50g piece of guanciale
  (cured pig's cheek)
  or smoked pancetta

2 cloves of garlic

2 sprigs of fresh rosemary

4 pork ribs (1kg total)

2 onions

2 sticks of celery

2 bulbs of fennel

200ml Frascati white wine

1 tablespoon tomato purée

2 x 400g tins of quality plum
  tomatoes

Joint the chicken (see page 386), then trim and finely slice the giblets, leaving the neck whole. Twist each sausage in the middle, then cut in half. Cover the porcini with boiling kettle water and leave to rehydrate. Roughly slice the guanciale, place in a large cold frying pan and put on a medium-low heat for a couple of minutes to render the fat. Peel the garlic and add the whole cloves to the pan with the rosemary sprigs. Start browning the ribs, then the chicken pieces, skin side down, turning until golden all over. As you go, transfer the meat to a large casserole pan on a low heat alongside, leaving the fat behind. Brown the sausages in the fat, also moving them to the casserole pan once coloured. Saving the liquor, add the porcini to the casserole pan with the giblets, then season with sea salt and black pepper. Preheat the oven to 160°C.

Peel and slice the onions and celery, and chop the fennel into wedges. Cook in the frying pan for 10 minutes, or until softened. Turn the meat pan up to high, pour in the wine, let it cook away, then add the veg, the porcini soaking water (discarding the last gritty bit) and the tomato purée. Scrunch in the tomatoes through your clean hands, then pour in 2 to 3 tins' worth of water to cover the meat by 1cm. Cover with a scrunched-up sheet of wet greaseproof paper and roast for 2 to 3 hours, or until really tender. Remove any bones, taste, and season to perfection. Great with Oozy polenta (see page 368), seasonal greens, pasta, bread or rice.

CALORIES	FAT	SAT FAT	PROTEIN	CARBS	SUGAR	SALT	FIBRE
492kcal	30.6g	10.5g	44g	7.8g	5.6g	1.7g	1.9g

SAFFRON CHICKEN

CRUNCHY GARLICKY ALMOND BREADCRUMBS, OREGANO & MARSALA

For me, this is a really sociable and delicious way to cook and serve chicken on the bone, bolstered by an incredible marinade. It's straightforward to put together but wonderfully diverse in flavour. You'll love it.

SERVES 4–6 | 1 HOUR 30 MINUTES, PLUS MARINATING

1 x 1.4kg whole chicken

1 good pinch of saffron

200ml Marsala wine

olive oil

600g ripe mixed-colour cherry tomatoes

1 bunch of fresh oregano (30g)

2 cloves of garlic

100g blanched almonds

100g stale rustic bread

Ideally you want to marinate your chicken the day before you cook it, for maximum flavour and juiciness. In a bowl, cover the saffron with a splash of boiling kettle water and leave for 2 minutes, then add the Marsala with 2 tablespoons of oil and a good pinch of sea salt and black pepper. Pour that into a large clean, plastic food bag, add the chicken, squeeze all the air out of the bag, tie a knot and give it a right little rub. Marinate in the fridge for at least 8 hours, preferably overnight, turning occasionally.

The next day, preheat the oven to 180°C. On a board, use a large sharp knife to carefully cut down the back of the chicken so you can open it out flat. Transfer the chicken (skin side up) and marinade to a roasting tray and place on the top shelf of the oven for 40 minutes. Meanwhile, put the tomatoes into a baking dish, pick in the oregano leaves, add 1 tablespoon of oil, season with salt and pepper, and toss to coat.

When the time's up, carefully put 2 tablespoons of fat from the chicken tray into a food processor. Peel and add the garlic, with the almonds. Tear in the bread and blitz into crumbs. Sprinkle and pat them all over the chicken. Return to the oven for a further 20 minutes, with the tomato dish beneath. I like to serve the chicken and all the crumbs on a big board, cutting it into chunks through the bone. Serve the tomatoes as they are, with a big green salad, or tossed through freshly cooked spaghetti.

CALORIES	FAT	SAT FAT	PROTEIN	CARBS	SUGAR	SALT	FIBRE
692kcal	41.8g	7.4g	48.5g	22.9g	9.4g	1.7g	2g

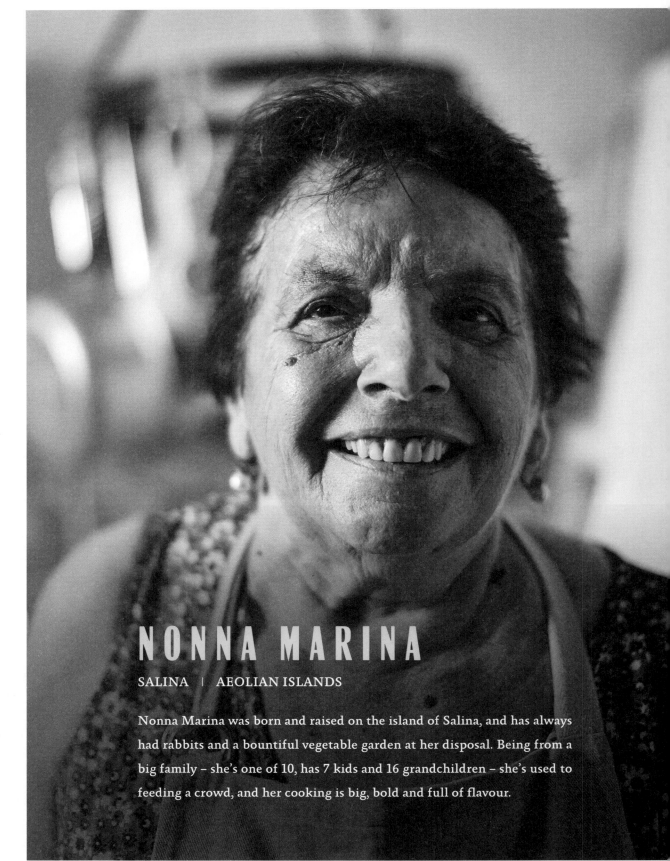

NONNA MARINA

SALINA | AEOLIAN ISLANDS

Nonna Marina was born and raised on the island of Salina, and has always had rabbits and a bountiful vegetable garden at her disposal. Being from a big family – she's one of 10, has 7 kids and 16 grandchildren – she's used to feeding a crowd, and her cooking is big, bold and full of flavour.

SWEET & SOUR RABBIT

BAY, ALMONDS & PINE NUTS

Nonna Marina uses bold ingredients and simple cooking methods to create big flavours. This recipe is inspired by a couple of delicious dishes that I was lucky enough to cook and enjoy with her, and I know you're going to love it – it's sticky, tender, and the unusual addition of nuts just works so well and adds a wonderful crunch. If you can't find rabbit, a jointed chicken will work a treat with these flavours, too.

SERVES 4 | 1 HOUR

1 whole rabbit (1.2kg),
  skinned, jointed, with offal

olive oil

1 red onion

5 ripe cherry tomatoes

1 fresh red chilli

5 fresh bay leaves

50g pine nuts

50g blanched almonds

½ teaspoon ground cloves

150ml full-bodied Sicilian
  red wine

100ml thick balsamic vinegar

1 tablespoon runny honey

Place all the rabbit and the offal in a cold casserole pan and add 3 tablespoons of oil. Put on a medium-high heat for the rabbit to get golden, turning occasionally, while you peel and finely slice the onion, quarter the tomatoes, then halve the chilli lengthways and deseed. Add it all to the pan with the bay, all the nuts, the cloves and wine. Pour in 350ml of water, bring to the boil, then simmer on a low heat for 15 minutes.

When the time's up, pour in the balsamic and add the honey. Cook for another 30 minutes, or until the rabbit is soft and tender and the liquid has reduced to a dark, thick, flavourful coating, stirring occasionally. Serve as is, or Marina serves hers at room temperature, which is common in hot climates like the Aeolian Islands. We had it with pasta, but it's also typical to enjoy it with couscous or bread. Delicious.

CALORIES	FAT	SAT FAT	PROTEIN	CARBS	SUGAR	SALT	FIBRE
580kcal	33g	6g	45.1g	19.7g	17.5g	0.3g	1g

FORAGER'S CHICKEN

MUSHROOMS, SMOKED PANCETTA, GARLIC, POTATOES, THYME & WINE

I dedicate this recipe to my favourite forager, Gennaro Contaldo. I can picture him eating this dish, tearing off bits of bread and mopping up all that delicious sauce. Making it is such fun – there's a really nice flow to the recipe and its time in the oven reduces it all down to a crispy, gnarly, tender and intense, gorgeous dinner.

SERVES 6 | 1 HOUR 45 MINUTES

20g dried porcini mushrooms

100g piece of smoked pancetta

olive oil

6 chicken legs

6 shallots

400g chestnut mushrooms

4 cloves of garlic

200ml Gavi di Gavi
   white wine

4 medium potatoes

4 sprigs of fresh thyme

200ml crème fraîche

Preheat the oven to 180°C. Crumble the dried porcini into a mug, fill it up with boiling water and put aside. Slice the pancetta into thick lardons, place in a large cold casserole pan with 1 tablespoon of oil and put the pan on a medium-high heat so the fat renders out. Once golden, scoop the pancetta into a large bowl, leaving the pan of fat on the heat.

Add the chicken legs to the fat in the pan, then peel and add the whole shallots. Turn the chicken legs until golden all over, then remove to the pancetta bowl with the shallots (you may need to work in batches). Halve or quarter the mushrooms, adding them to the pan as you go. Toss until lightly golden while you peel and finely slice the garlic. Stir the garlic into the pan and fry until lightly golden, then pour in the wine and let it reduce by half. Peel, dice and stir in the potatoes, then return the chicken, shallots and pancetta to the pan, along with any juices from the bowl.

Pour in the porcini and their soaking water (discarding just the last gritty bit), then tie the thyme sprigs together and add to the pan. Place in the oven for 1 hour, or until cooked through, basting every 20 minutes. At this point, the sauce should have reduced nicely, so spoon in the crème fraîche and return to the oven for a final 5 minutes to let the flavours mingle.

CALORIES	FAT	SAT FAT	PROTEIN	CARBS	SUGAR	SALT	FIBRE
672kcal	45.2g	17.7g	41.2g	21g	2.5g	1g	3g

FISH

NONNA MARIA

PROCIDA | NAPLES

Nonna Maria is the island's only fisherwoman and has been cooking her whole life. She used to go fishing with her father, and after he passed away she'd go with her fisherman husband, so it's always been her way of life. She still fishes every day, cooking her catch for her family, or for village festivals and celebrations. What a woman.

FISH IN CRAZY WATER

ACQUA PAZZA – THE ULTIMATE ISLAND FISH DISH

~~~~~~

I'm excited to share this fantastic method that shows just how easy it can be to cook whole fish, on the bone, giving better flavour and succulence, plus it's harder to overcook the fish and you should also find it's better value. Everything really gives to everything on the flavour front in this dish – it's a beautiful thing!

SERVES 2 | 30 MINUTES

2 spring onions

½ a bulb of fennel

1 carrot

200g ripe mixed-colour cherry tomatoes, on the vine

3 cloves of garlic

½ a fresh red chilli

8–10 mixed olives (stone in)

olive oil

2 x 350g whole round fish, such as royal bream, trout, sea bass, red mullet, scaled, gutted, gills removed

1 bunch of mixed fresh soft herbs (30g), such as flat-leaf parsley, mint, fennel tops

150ml Greco di Tufo white wine

1 lemon

extra virgin olive oil

Trim the spring onions and fennel (reserving any leafy tops), peel the carrot, then slice them all ½cm thick. Halve the tomatoes. Peel and finely slice the garlic and chilli. Squash and destone the olives. Put a large frying pan on a high heat with 1 tablespoon of olive oil. Stir in the onions, fennel and carrot, followed 4 minutes later by the tomatoes, garlic, chilli and olives. Toss regularly for 2 minutes while you lightly score the fish on both sides (this will help flavour and heat to penetrate as it cooks).

Lay the fish on top of the veg, stuff half the herbs into the cavities, then pour over the wine and let it reduce by half. Add about 300ml of water, to come 1cm up the side of the pan. Cover and leave to thunder away on a high heat for 8 minutes (boiling underneath, steaming on top means fragrant veggies). Pick the remaining herb leaves, finely grate the lemon zest over them, then chop and mix together.

Uncover the fish and baste with its juices for 1 minute. To check the fish is cooked, go to the thickest part up near the head – if the flesh flakes easily away from the bone, it's done. Remove to a plate, spoon over the veg and juices, drizzle with extra virgin olive oil, scatter over the lemony herbs, then squeeze over the lemon juice. Great served with bread to mop up that irresistible sauce, or with new potatoes, couscous or rice.

CALORIES	FAT	SAT FAT	PROTEIN	CARBS	SUGAR	SALT	FIBRE
407kcal	17.3g	1.6g	40.3g	11.6g	10.1g	0.8g	3.3g

CUTTLEFISH & POTATO STEW

SPICY 'NDUJA, FENNEL, RED WINE & PARSLEY

This is a really different, delicious, comforting stew. Before you say, 'Where on earth am I going to get cuttlefish?' – they're often a bycatch and in abundance in British waters and many other places around the world. Any half-decent fishmonger will order them for you, or you can swap in large squid instead.

SERVES 6 | 2 HOURS 15 MINUTES

50g 'nduja

2 lemons

olive oil

4 medium cuttlefish, cleaned, trimmed, with tentacles, heads removed (1.4kg total)

2 red onions

2 cloves of garlic

2 bulbs of fennel

250ml Primitivo red wine

1kg potatoes

1 x 400g tin of quality cherry tomatoes

extra virgin olive oil

½ a bunch of fresh flat-leaf parsley (15g)

In a pestle and mortar, smash the 'nduja into a paste, then muddle in the juice of 1 lemon and an equal amount of olive oil. Halve each cuttlefish body lengthways, score the insides in a criss-cross fashion at 1cm intervals, then rub inside and out with the 'nduja mix. Marinate in the fridge.

Meanwhile, cut the cuttlefish tentacles into pieces and place in a large casserole pan on a medium-high heat with 2 tablespoons of olive oil. Cook for 10 minutes, stirring occasionally, while you peel the onions and garlic, trim the fennel, then roughly chop it all. Pour the wine into the pan and let it reduce by half, using a wooden spoon to scrape up the sticky bits from the base of the pan, then stir in the chopped veg. Cook for 30 minutes, or until caramelized, stirring regularly and adding splashes of water, if needed. Peel the potatoes and chop into 3cm chunks, then stir into the pan with the tomatoes and cover with 1 litre of water. Bring to the boil, then simmer, uncovered, for 1 hour, or until everything is tender, stirring occasionally.

Cook the marinated cuttlefish in a screaming hot griddle pan, or on your barbecue, for 1 minute on each side, or until lightly charred all over. Remove to a board, finely slice with the top leafy half of your parsley, then toss through the stew with a drizzle of extra virgin olive oil and a squeeze of lemon juice. Have a taste, season to perfection, and serve.

CALORIES	FAT	SAT FAT	PROTEIN	CARBS	SUGAR	SALT	FIBRE
480kcal	14.5g	2.6g	44.7g	38.1g	8.3g	2.6g	6.2g

GOLDEN BREADED TUNA

AEOLIAN SPAGHETTI WITH LEMON, CAPERS, PECORINO, CHILLI & HERBS

Milanese has been one of my favourite things to eat ever since I was a kid. This version is really breaking the rules but on the islands it's all about fish, so I wanted to recreate that Milanese vibe, teaming a super-simple yet flavour-packed pasta with a beautifully cooked piece of fresh tuna. With good fish, cooking it rare is delicious, but Jools prefers it cooked a bit more. Do whatever makes you happy – just don't overcook it.

SERVES 2 | 15 MINUTES

1 tablespoon baby capers in brine

150g dried spaghetti

2 x 150g super-fresh yellowfin tuna steaks (ideally 2cm thick)

1 large egg

50g stale sourdough breadcrumbs

1 clove of garlic

1 fresh red chilli

3 sprigs of fresh flat-leaf parsley

3 sprigs of fresh mint

30g pecorino or Parmesan cheese

1 lemon

olive oil

Soak the capers in a bowl of water. Cook the pasta in a pan of boiling salted water according to the packet instructions. Meanwhile, season the tuna all over with sea salt and black pepper. Whip the egg in a shallow bowl. Put the breadcrumbs on a plate. Dunk the tuna in the egg, let any excess drip off, then dip each side in the crumbs to coat. Peel the garlic and finely slice with the chilli. Pick and finely chop the herb leaves. Finely grate the pecorino, then half the lemon zest, keeping them separate.

Place a large and a medium frying pan on a medium-high heat. Once hot, place 1 tablespoon of oil and the breaded tuna in the medium pan, turning after 1 to 2 minutes, or when golden, then remove to a board, leaving the tuna rare throughout. Alongside, fry the garlic, chilli, drained capers and lemon zest with 1 tablespoon of oil in the large pan, stirring regularly.

Drain the pasta, reserving a mugful of starchy cooking water. Toss into the large pan, squeeze in half the lemon juice, and loosen with a little of the reserved cooking water. Toss in the herbs and pecorino until you get a silky, shiny sauce, loosening with more cooking water, if needed. Taste, season to perfection and promptly divide between your plates. Halve the tuna, sit it on top and serve with lemon wedges, for squeezing over.

CALORIES	FAT	SAT FAT	PROTEIN	CARBS	SUGAR	SALT	FIBRE
745kcal	29.7g	7.8g	53.8g	69.5g	3.6g	1.5g	2.6g

NONNA FRANCHINA

SALINA | AEOLIAN ISLANDS

Nonna Franchina is a remarkable woman. I met her picking capers on her farm, which is also her backyard. At the ripe old age of 92, I think that's pretty incredible. Franchina has been cooking since the age of 10, so she has a wealth of experience. The old-school methods she showed me – like using needle and thread to seal her stuffed squid – were really quite inspiring and a reminder that cooking should be practical. Franchina said that if I liked her recipe, I should tell everyone about it, which would make her very happy. So please keep it alive and cook it from the pages that follow.

STUFFED BRAISED SQUID

CAPERS, BREADCRUMBS, PECORINO, GARLIC & PARSLEY

Salina is known for its capers, and as her family have grown them for generations, Nonna Franchina is totally in tune with how to make the most of them in her cooking. This dish is a wonderfully tasty example of that.

SERVES 4 | 1 HOUR

25g baby capers in brine

100g coarse stale breadcrumbs

1 large egg

olive oil

15g pecorino or Parmesan cheese, plus extra to serve

1 clove of garlic

½ a bunch of fresh flat-leaf parsley (15g)

1 red onion

10 ripe cherry tomatoes

1 x 680g jar of passata

4 medium squid, cleaned, gutted (300g total)

300g dried spaghetti

2 sprigs of fresh basil

Place half the capers in a bowl with the breadcrumbs, egg, 1 tablespoon of oil and 2 tablespoons of water. Finely grate in the pecorino, peel the garlic, finely chop with the parsley (stalks and all), then scrunch it all together.

Peel and finely slice the onion and place in a casserole pan on a medium heat with 2 tablespoons of oil, stirring occasionally. Now, a great nonna trick: squeeze the tomatoes while submerged in a bowl of water to remove the seeds (and prevent them going everywhere!). Add the tomatoes to the pan with the passata. Simmer on a low heat while you stuff the squid.

Keeping the tentacles to one side, just over half-fill each squid tube with the breadcrumb mixture, pushing it right down into the tube but being mindful not to pack it too tightly. Use a cocktail stick or toothpick to seal or, like Franchina learnt from her grandparents, use a needle and thread. Stir the remaining capers into the sauce, then add the stuffed squid and tentacles. Simmer on a low heat for 25 to 30 minutes, or until tender.

Meanwhile, cook the pasta in a pan of boiling salted water according to the packet instructions. Use tongs to move the squid pieces to a board. Removing the sticks or thread, slice the tubes to reveal the filling, then arrange on a platter, spoon over a little sauce and pick over the basil. Drain the pasta, reserving a mugful of starchy cooking water, then toss with the remaining sauce, loosening with a splash of cooking water, if needed. Serve with a grating of pecorino, alongside that tasty braised squid.

CALORIES	FAT	SAT FAT	PROTEIN	CARBS	SUGAR	SALT	FIBRE
577kcal	16.1g	3.1g	28.1g	83.9g	15g	1.8g	5.4g

SUMMER FISH STEW

BREAD, PEAS & GARLIC AÏOLI

~~~~~~

A wonderfully luxurious meal, this colourful one-pot wonder celebrates fish and seafood with flavours that always blow my mind. It's fun to make and flexible, meaning you can use whatever is available to you.

SERVES 4 | 40 MINUTES

1 x Garlic aïoli (see page 374)

1 onion

1 clove of garlic

1 stick of celery

1 large potato

1 fresh red chilli

½ a bunch of fresh flat-leaf parsley (15g)

olive oil

150ml Prosecco

1 x 680g jar of passata

2 large bream fillets, scaled, pin-boned

4 langoustines, shell on

400g mixed mussels & clams, scrubbed, debearded

200g squid tubes, cleaned

100g freshly podded peas

4 thick slices of rustic bread

Make your Garlic aïoli (see page 374). Peel the onion, garlic, celery (picking and saving any yellow leaves from the head) and potato. Finely chop the onion and garlic with the chilli (deseed, if you like) and parsley stalks (reserving the leaves). Chop the celery and potato into 1cm chunks. Place it all in a large casserole pan on a medium heat with 2 tablespoons of oil, and cook for 10 minutes, or until softened, stirring occasionally.

Stir in the Prosecco and let it simmer for 2 minutes. Pour in the passata and half a jar's worth of water, add a good pinch of sea salt and black pepper, then add the bream and langoustines, pushing them down into the sauce. Simmer gently while you quickly pick through the mussels and clams, tapping any open ones – if they don't close, discard them. Finely slice the squid into rings. Add the mussels, clams, squid and peas to the pan with a splash of water, if needed, then cover and leave for a few minutes, or until the mussels and clams have opened (discard any that remain closed).

Place a slice of bread in each of your bowls (toast first, if you like), ladle the stew on top, dollop each portion with ½ a tablespoon of aïoli (saving the rest for another day), then tear over the reserved parsley and any celery leaves. If you've got them, fennel tops are a lovely finishing touch, too.

CALORIES	FAT	SAT FAT	PROTEIN	CARBS	SUGAR	SALT	FIBRE
581kcal	18.7g	2.3g	45.2g	55g	15.4g	2.7g	6.1g

GRILLED SQUID SALAD

ISLAND SALSA OF CAPERS, PISTACHIOS, CHILLI, MINT & LEMON

~~~~~~

Inspired by the investment in flavour that Nonna Franchina made in stuffing her squid, I came up with this recipe, which uses the same principle but in reverse. We're making a mind-blowing salsa to plunge the hot grilled squid straight into, creating a wonderful harmony between flavour and texture. The salsa is also great when used to dress grilled veg, lamb or other seafood, tossed with pasta or as a topping for crostini.

SERVES 4-6 | 30 MINUTES

2 tablespoons baby capers in brine

2 lemons

extra virgin olive oil

1 clove of garlic

1 fresh red chilli

4 anchovy fillets in oil

30g shelled unsalted pistachios

½ a bunch of fresh mint (15g)

4 large squid, cleaned, gutted

500g large ripe tomatoes

Soak the capers in a bowl of water. Squeeze all the lemon juice into a large shallow bowl and add 4 tablespoons of oil. Peel the garlic and finely chop with the chilli, anchovies, pistachios, drained capers and mint leaves. Scrape it all into the bowl and mix together well.

Reserving the tentacles, run a sharp knife down the length of each squid tube, cutting through one side only so you can open each one out like a book. Lightly score the inside of each tube in a criss-cross fashion at ½cm intervals. To cook the squid, follow Franchina's guidance and get the tentacles on early, then add the tubes, from largest to smallest. In a screaming hot griddle pan or on a barbecue, cook each piece for about 1 minute per side – with no oil or seasoning – until lightly charred and starting to curl. Start with the cut side when you do the tubes, and keep the squid moving for even cooking. As each piece is done, use tongs to dunk it straight into the salsa, turning and coating it in all that flavour.

Slice the tomatoes and lay over a serving platter. Finely slice the squid tubes, pull the tentacles apart, then arrange on top of the tomatoes. Spoon over all the remaining salsa, and serve hot or at room temperature.

CALORIES	FAT	SAT FAT	PROTEIN	CARBS	SUGAR	SALT	FIBRE
266kcal	18.4g	2.8g	19g	6.5g	4.7g	0.9g	1.8g

WHOLE ROASTED SEA BASS

FENNEL, OLIVE & SWEET ORANGE SALAD

Roasting a whole large fish like this is such a treat, but you can easily use two smaller fish instead, which will be just as delicious. As the fish bakes, its natural juices blend beautifully with the vermouth, to create amazingly fragrant flavour. Teamed with the salad, it's a brilliantly fresh plate of food. We serve it just like this at home, or for even more of a treat, we sometimes roast some potato chips to enjoy on the side.

SERVES 8 | 45 MINUTES

3 large bulbs of fennel, ideally with leafy tops attached

1 bunch of mixed fresh soft herbs (30g), such as fennel tops, marjoram, parsley

1 x 2kg or 2 x 1kg whole sea bass, scaled, gutted, gills removed

1 large red onion

olive oil

250ml vermouth

2 knobs of unsalted butter

5 regular or blood oranges

red wine vinegar

5 black olives (stone in)

extra virgin olive oil

Preheat the oven to full whack (240°C). Finely slice the fennel stalks, stopping when you hit the bulb, and reserving the leafy tops. Stuff the sliced stalks and the herbs inside the cavity of the fish. Peel and finely slice the onion, then scatter half of it into an oiled roasting tray, large enough to fit the fish snugly. Sit the fish upright in the tray, bending it to fit, if needed. Season from a height with sea salt and black pepper, pour over the vermouth and 2 tablespoons of olive oil, add the butter, then squeeze over the juice of 1 orange. Place in the hot oven, then immediately reduce the temperature to 180°C. Roast for 30 minutes (20 minutes for 2 smaller fish), or until cooked to perfection, basting twice. To check the fish is cooked, go to the thickest part up near the head – if the flesh flakes easily away from the bone, it's done.

Meanwhile, scrunch the remaining sliced onion in a little vinegar to quickly pickle it. Very finely slice the fennel bulbs, and sprinkle over a serving platter with any reserved leafy tops. Top and tail the remaining oranges, cut off the peel, then slice into rounds and arrange on the platter.

When you're ready to serve, scatter the quick-pickled onion over the salad. Squash, destone and tear over the olives, then drizzle everything from a height with extra virgin olive oil, season to taste and gently toss together. Serve the salad and fish at the table, drizzling each portion of fish with some of those flavoursome juices from the tray before tucking in.

CALORIES	FAT	SAT FAT	PROTEIN	CARBS	SUGAR	SALT	FIBRE
397kcal	23.6g	6.5g	32.1g	9.7g	9.1g	0.4g	1g

TURBOT AL FORNO

PANCETTA, POTATOES, MUSHROOMS, CHERRY TOMATOES, RED ONION & ROSEMARY

I regularly cook traybakes like this, where the dish you end up with is greater than the sum of its parts. The fish flavours all the other ingredients as it cooks, and vice versa. Cooking fish steaks on the bone is a revelation – it's more meaty and you get better flavour and juiciness. Round fish steaks are called darnes, and flatfish steaks, which I'm celebrating here, are called tranches, so that's what you need to ask your fishmonger for. Turbot, brill and halibut are never cheap, but well worth it for a treat.

SERVES 2 | 1 HOUR 10 MINUTES

400g potatoes

4 cloves of garlic

1 red onion

2 thick-cut rashers of smoked
  pancetta or streaky bacon

10 ripe cherry tomatoes

2 sprigs of fresh rosemary

olive oil

2 x 300g tranches of flatfish,
  such as turbot, brill,
  halibut, skin on

150g girolle or other
  mushrooms

1 lemon

½ a fresh red chilli

20g wild rocket

extra virgin olive oil

Preheat the oven to 180°C. Peel the potatoes and slice 1cm thick, then place in a roasting tray or dish (20cm x 30cm). Lightly squash and add the whole unpeeled garlic cloves, then peel, finely slice and add the onion. Chop the pancetta into chunky lardons, add to the tray with the tomatoes, strip over the rosemary leaves and drizzle with olive oil. Season well, toss to coat, then arrange in a flat layer. Roast for 25 minutes.

Meanwhile, wash the fish, pat dry with kitchen paper, then place in a bowl. Clean and tear over the larger mushrooms, leaving small ones whole, season with sea salt and black pepper, drizzle with 1 tablespoon of olive oil and squeeze over half the lemon juice to give it a quick marinade. When the time's up on the potatoes, nestle the fish into the tray, scatter over the mushrooms, and return to the oven to roast for another 25 minutes, or until the fish is just cooked through.

Deseed and very finely slice the chilli, then scatter over with the rocket. Finish with a drizzle of extra virgin olive oil, and serve with lemon wedges.

CALORIES	FAT	SAT FAT	PROTEIN	CARBS	SUGAR	SALT	FIBRE
462kcal	14.2g	2.9g	40.7g	45.6g	8.6g	1g	5.9g

NONNA ROSANNA

CATANIA | SICILY

Nonna Rosanna is a force to be reckoned with. Having visited the Pescheria fish market for more than 50 years, since she was a young child accompanying her fishmonger father, she knows exactly how to suss out the good fish from the dodgy stuff, and everyone knows who she is. Rosanna is the gatekeeper of her mother's recipes and stays true to the methods she's learnt. Cooking with her was a real masterclass in depth of flavour. Her dishes are like camouflage – they don't necessarily look like much but when you taste them they smash your expectations. See for yourself on the pages that follow.

UGLY BEAUTIFUL TUNA

SWEET & SOUR SLOW-COOKED ONIONS

This is one of the most delicious, yet ugly, dishes I've ever seen, tasted or cooked, and that's why I had to put it in the book. The flavour is extraordinary, created – just as Nonna Rosanna says – by cooking with love and elbow grease. Using cheap ingredients, in this case onions, and cooking them with utter dedication can still give rich flavour. Rosanna used belly of tuna, which is cheaper in Italy, but you can use any cut.

SERVES 4 | 50 MINUTES

4 onions

olive oil

4 x 150g yellowfin tuna steaks
   (ideally 2cm thick)

3 tablespoons red wine
   vinegar

Peel and finely slice the onions, then rinse them in a large bowl of water – Rosanna does this to make the onions milder. Place your largest frying pan on a medium-low heat, then briefly drain the onions and add them to the pan. Season well with sea salt, then cover and steam for 15 minutes.

Drizzle 6 tablespoons of oil into the pan, and cover again so you get that balance between steaming and frying. Cook for another 15 minutes, or until the onions are caramelized, stirring regularly. You want to get sticky bits at the base of the pan – that's how you know they're getting really good. Remove the lid and push the onions to one side of the pan, then add the tuna, in batches if you need to, turning and cooking for 2 minutes on each side for blushing pink, 3 to 4 minutes each side for cooked through.

Transfer the tuna to a serving platter. Add the vinegar to the pan, let it cook away, then stir in a splash of water to pick up all the sticky bits. Spoon the onions over the tuna. Delicious served hot – though Rosanna recommends serving this at room temperature – with a fresh zesty salad.

CALORIES	FAT	SAT FAT	PROTEIN	CARBS	SUGAR	SALT	FIBRE
444kcal	26.6g	4.6g	37.4g	14.4g	11.2g	0.7g	4g

AMAZING OCTOPUS

POACHED IN ITS OWN JUICES & SEARED UNTIL CRISPY

Octopus is becoming incredibly trendy in restaurants now, and while it may seem daunting to consider cooking one at home, it's well worth a go. The ritual is one to embrace, giving you extremely tender meat, sticky bits and an extraordinary broth, all of which have lots of tasty possibilities for future meals.

SERVES 8 | 1 HOUR 20 MINUTES

1 large octopus (2kg), cleaned, beak removed

olive oil

3 cloves of garlic

1 fresh red chilli

6 anchovy fillets in oil

200g ripe cherry tomatoes

1 bunch of fresh flat-leaf parsley (30g)

2 tablespoons balsamic vinegar

Plunge the octopus into a very large, deep pan of boiling water (no salt – this is very important!) for 2 minutes to clean it, then lift out on to a large plate (it will curl up slightly). Pour the water away, then place the pan back on a medium-low heat with 6 tablespoons of oil. Peel the garlic and finely slice with the chilli, then fry them gently with the anchovies until softened but not coloured, stirring occasionally.

Pull the octopus tentacles up around the head, then add it to the pan, followed by the tomatoes and parsley (stalks and all). Cover and cook for 35 minutes, or until tender – lots of amazing juice will come out of the octopus, giving you the most incredible broth for soups and pastas. Turn the heat off and leave the octopus to sit for 15 minutes in its juices.

Remove the octopus to a board. Sieve and reserve the delicious broth (you may want to dilute it with a little extra water to balance the saltiness). Save the thick sticky mixture left behind in the sieve. Cut off the octopus tentacles, halve the head and body, then sear it all in a large hot pan with 2 tablespoons of oil for a few minutes on each side, or until golden all over.

Transfer the octopus and any cooking juices to a bowl and drizzle over the balsamic. You can eat it right away, or it will keep in the fridge for up to 2 days. Turn the page for four delicious ways I love to serve and enjoy it.

CALORIES	FAT	SAT FAT	PROTEIN	CARBS	SUGAR	SALT	FIBRE
343kcal	16.7g	2.7g	45.8g	2.7g	2.3g	0.2g	0.5g

OCTOPUS 4 WAYS

SALAD, PASTA, BRUSCHETTA, SOUP

All of these dishes celebrate the joy of poached, seared octopus (see page 266), and are well worth a try.

OCTOPUS SALAD

SERVES 2 | 10 MINUTES

Peel and very finely slice **½ a red onion**. Speed-peel **4 delicate sticks of celery** into ribbons (reserving any yellow leaves). Finely slice **½–1 fresh red chilli** at an angle, and pick most of the leaves from **½ a bunch of fresh flat-leaf parsley (15g)**. Season it all from a height with sea salt and black pepper, drizzle with a little **red wine vinegar** and **extra virgin olive oil**, and gently toss together. Arrange nicely on a serving platter. Finely slice **250g of seared octopus**, then mix into the salad. Scatter over any reserved celery leaves and the remaining parsley leaves. Squeeze over a little **lemon juice**, to taste, and serve.

OCTOPUS PASTA

SERVES 2 | 15 MINUTES

Cook **150g of dried pasta** in a pan of boiling salted water according to the packet instructions. Meanwhile, finely slice **2 cloves of garlic** and place in a frying pan on a medium-high heat with **1 tablespoon of olive oil** and **1 handful of ripe cherry tomatoes**. Fry for 4 minutes, or until softened, tossing regularly, while you chop **250g of seared octopus**. Stir it into the frying pan with **1 ladleful of the broth**. When the pasta's done, scoop it into the pan, tear in the leaves from **½ a bunch of fresh flat-leaf parsley (15g)** and toss well, loosening with a little pasta cooking water, if needed.

OCTOPUS BRUSCHETTA

SERVES 2 | 10 MINUTES

Warm the **thick sticky mixture** you saved in a pan on a low heat with a splash of **broth**, mashing as you go. Finely chop and add any **leftover octopus**, then spoon over hot **garlic-rubbed toasts** and top with a few **fresh parsley leaves**. Serve with a drizzle of **extra virgin olive oil** and **lemon wedges**, if you like.

OCTOPUS SOUP

SERVES 2 | 15 MINUTES

Sieve **350ml of beautiful octopus broth** into a pan with 350ml of boiling water, then drop in **150g of dried pasta** and cook according to the packet instructions. Taste and season to perfection, drizzle with a little **extra virgin olive oil**, and finish with a sprinkling of finely ground **dried red chilli flakes**.

NONNA HALU

NOMENTANO | ROME

I had the honour of joining Nonna Halu and her family for one of their weekly Shabbat feasts, cooking and learning about how their traditional food and culture have been both influenced by and blended with the flavours and spirit of Rome. Halu and her family fled Libya more than 50 years ago without a penny to their name, to seek refuge in Rome, where there's now a settled community of Libyan Jews. With them comes their heritage, and the things that remind us of home often revolve around food and the dinner table. Cook her lovely fish stew from the pages that follow.

LIBYAN FISH STEW

MINTY COUSCOUS & TOASTED CUMIN

The spices that Nonna Halu and her family use are very particular. She showed me her signature dish, an incredible fish stew, and I've tried to recreate that as best I could for you here. It's wonderfully flavoursome.

SERVES 4 | 55 MINUTES

4 cloves of garlic

2 red onions

1 fresh red chilli

olive oil

1 teaspoon ground cumin

1 teaspoon caraway seeds

2 tablespoons tomato purée

2 teaspoons rose harissa

2 lemons

4 x 200g darnes of grouper, scaled

300g couscous

1 tablespoon cumin seeds

1 bunch of fresh mint (30g)

Peel and finely chop the garlic and onions, finely slice the chilli, then place it all in a large pan on a medium heat with 2 tablespoons of oil. Cook for 10 minutes, or until just starting to caramelize, stirring occasionally. Add the ground cumin and the caraway, then, 3 minutes later, the tomato purée and harissa. Finely grate in the zest of 1 lemon, squeeze in its juice, add 750ml of water and stir well. Boil, then cover and simmer on a low heat for 20 minutes, or until slightly reduced, removing the lid halfway.

Season the fish on both sides with sea salt, then place in the sauce (using darnes gives your sauce bonus flavour from the bones as the fish cooks, but you can use fillets, if you prefer). Cover and cook for 12 to 15 minutes, or until tender, basting with the sauce halfway. Meanwhile, place the couscous in a bowl, just cover with boiling kettle water, pop a plate on top and leave to fluff up. Toast the cumin seeds in a dry frying pan until golden. Pick and finely chop the mint leaves, reserving the baby ones.

Stir the chopped mint through the couscous, then taste and season to perfection. Serve the couscous and fish stew sprinkled with toasted cumin seeds and baby mint leaves, with lemon wedges for squeezing over.

CALORIES	FAT	SAT FAT	PROTEIN	CARBS	SUGAR	SALT	FIBRE
720kcal	28.9g	5.5g	51.9g	69.4g	9.2g	0.9g	5.7g

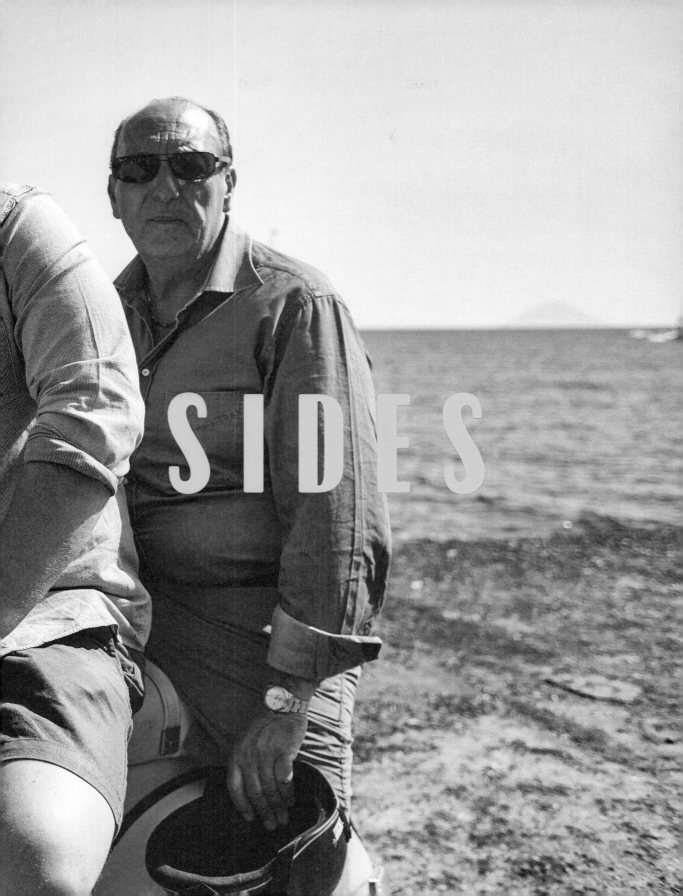

SIDES

POT-ROAST CAULIFLOWER

SWEET ONIONS, ANCHOVIES, OLIVES & WHITE WINE

This spectacular dish really heroes and focuses on the incredibleness of a big, fat, juicy cauliflower. It's given the time, love and care you'd give to a prime cut of meat, which allows this dish to be a fantastic side dish, an amazing starter with toasted bread, or indeed a main course in its own right, served with bread, rice or pasta.

SERVES 4-8 | 2 HOURS

3 onions

olive oil

6 anchovy fillets in oil

6 cloves of garlic

6 large green olives (stone in)

500ml Gavi di Gavi white wine

optional: 1 small pinch of saffron

1 large head of cauliflower, with leaves

Preheat the oven to 180°C. Peel and quarter the onions, then pick the quarters apart into petals straight into a 20cm-wide, deep ovenproof pan on a medium-high heat. Add 1 tablespoon of olive oil and the anchovies and stir occasionally while you peel and slice the garlic. Squash the olives, leaving the stones in, then stir into the pan with the garlic. Cook and stir for 2 minutes, then pour in the wine and add the saffron, if using.

Trim the base of the cauliflower, then use a sharp knife to carefully score a deep cross into the stalk. Remove only any tatty outer leaves, leaving the rest intact. Sit the cauliflower in the pan, stalk side down, and drizzle with 1 tablespoon of oil. Spoon some of the onions and liquid over the cauliflower, then bring to the boil and carefully transfer the pan to the oven for 1 hour 30 minutes, or until the cauliflower is tender (check by inserting a sharp knife). Baste it with the pan juices twice during cooking.

Carefully lift the cauliflower on to a platter and spoon over the soft onions, olives and fragrant juices from the pan. Slice, and serve.

CALORIES	FAT	SAT FAT	PROTEIN	CARBS	SUGAR	SALT	FIBRE
260kcal	9g	1.4g	8.6g	17.2g	13g	0.8g	6g

CARROT CAPONATA

PINE NUTS, SWEET RAISINS & ONIONS, SOUR VINEGAR

This is a surprisingly delicious dish that really makes a hero of carrots, which are too often thought of as a bog-standard vegetable. Cooked like this they're the star of the show and, probably, of the whole meal. Serve this hot or cold, as a side dish or antipasto, with cold meats, cheeses and bread, or with rocket as a nice salad.

SERVES 8 | 1 HOUR 20 MINUTES

2 red onions

2 cloves of garlic

2 fresh red chillies

olive oil

1kg mixed-colour baby
  heritage carrots

50g pine nuts

50g raisins

2 tablespoons runny honey

4 tablespoons red wine
  vinegar

Peel and roughly slice the onions and garlic. Halve the chillies lengthways and deseed. Place it all in a large frying pan on a medium heat with 6 tablespoons of oil, stirring regularly. Wash, trim and add the carrots, along with the pine nuts, raisins and a pinch of sea salt. Cook for around 1 hour, or until the carrots are soft and beginning to caramelize (the time will vary depending on their size). Stir regularly and add little splashes of water as you go to prevent them from sticking, if needed.

Drizzle in the honey and vinegar and stir well. Cook for another 5 minutes, or until glossy and slightly sticky. Taste, season to perfection, and enjoy.

CALORIES	FAT	SAT FAT	PROTEIN	CARBS	SUGAR	SALT	FIBRE
225kcal	14.5g	1.8g	2.4g	22.2g	20.7g	0.3g	4.1g

AMAZING ROAST VEG
AUBERGINES, PEPPERS, COURGETTES, FENNEL

~~~~~~

Every vegetable can be extraordinarily delicious. Think of the beyond-simple methods below as principles you can take and embellish however you like. It's about dressing each veg with good oil, seasoning, a specific herb and acid, and maybe adding a curveball ingredient like garlic, capers or olives, then letting the oven do the work. With each mouthful, you'll get clear, definitive, exciting flavours. Enjoy as a side for meat or fish, tossed with salad or pasta, as part of an antipasti spread, or even added to stews at the last minute.

EACH SERVES 4 | APPROX. 1 HOUR

AUBERGINES Preheat the oven to 180°C. Cut **2 large aubergines (400g each)** lengthways into chunky wedges and place in a roasting tray. Peel **1 clove of garlic** and pound with **1 pinch each of dried red chilli flakes**, sea salt and black pepper in a pestle and mortar. Muddle in **4 tablespoons each of olive oil and red wine vinegar**. Use **½ a bunch of fresh thyme (15g)** to brush the dressing over the aubergines, reserving the thyme. Roast in a single layer for 45 minutes, scattering over the thyme for an extra 10 minutes, or until soft.

PEPPERS Preheat the oven to 180°C. Slice **4 mixed-colour peppers** into quarters, removing the seeds. Strip the leaves from **1 sprig of fresh oregano** into a pestle and mortar with a pinch of sea salt and black pepper and pound into a paste. Muddle in **4 tablespoons each of olive oil and white wine vinegar**, then peel and finely slice **2 cloves of garlic**, and mix into the dressing with **25g of baby capers**. In a roasting tray, toss the dressing with the peppers, arrange in a single layer, then roast for 45 minutes to 1 hour, or until soft.

COURGETTES Preheat the oven to 180°C. Pick the leaves from **½ a bunch of fresh basil (15g)** into a pestle and mortar, add a pinch of sea salt and pound into a paste. Muddle in **4 tablespoons of olive oil** and the juice of **1 lemon**, then finely slice and add **1 fresh red chilli**. Roughly chop **4 mixed-colour courgettes**, toss with the dressing in a roasting tray, then roast in a single layer for 45 minutes to 1 hour, or until soft.

FENNEL Preheat the oven to 180°C. Squash and destone **12 black olives**. Mix with **4 tablespoons of olive oil**, the juice of **1 lemon**, **1 pinch of dried red chilli flakes** and **1 teaspoon of fennel seeds**, then taste and season to perfection. Cut **2 bulbs of fennel** lengthways into 8 wedges. Toss the fennel with the dressing and **1 quartered lemon** in a roasting tray, arrange in a single layer, cover with tin foil and roast for 30 minutes, then uncover and roast for another 30 minutes. Carefully squeeze over the roasted lemon juice, to serve.

ASPARAGUS

SMASHED ALMOND, SUN-DRIED TOMATO & PECORINO PESTO

The simple act of making your own pesto is such a pleasurable one – it gives a pungency and elegance in flavour that you never quite get from a jar. Enjoy this alongside roasted or grilled meat or fish or even as a lunch or starter. The pesto is also great with artichokes, purple sprouting broccoli, sea kale or baby courgettes.

SERVES 4 | 25 MINUTES

2 lemons

½ a clove of garlic

50g blanched almonds

50g sun-dried tomatoes

1 bunch of fresh basil (30g)

extra virgin olive oil

30g pecorino or Parmesan cheese

2 bunches of asparagus (700g total)

Finely grate the zest of 1 lemon into a pestle and mortar. Peel and add the garlic, along with the almonds and sun-dried tomatoes. Pound really well into a paste – put some welly into it! Reserving the baby basil leaves, pick the rest into the mortar and bash well, then muddle in 4 tablespoons of oil and the juice of 1 lemon. Finely grate in most of the pecorino, mix together, taste, and season to perfection with sea salt and black pepper.

Snap off and discard the woody ends of the asparagus, then cook the spears for about 3 minutes in a pan of fast-boiling salted water on a high heat. Drain and divide between your plates. Add a spoonful of pesto to each portion, then finely grate over the remaining pecorino and sprinkle over the reserved basil leaves. Serve with lemon wedges for squeezing over. Any leftover pesto will keep happily in the fridge for up to 3 days.

CALORIES	FAT	SAT FAT	PROTEIN	CARBS	SUGAR	SALT	FIBRE
323kcal	28.9g	4.8g	10.1g	5.8g	4.5g	0.7g	3.1g

CHICKPEAS

SERVES 6–8 | 50 MINUTES

Finely slice the white half of **1 leek** (save the green part for another recipe). Place in a large pan on a low heat with **2 tablespoons each of olive oil** and water. Cook for 15 minutes, stirring regularly. Tip in **2 x 700g jars of fat chickpeas** (juice and all), then pour in half a jar's worth of water and turn the heat up to medium. Peel and add **4 whole cloves of garlic**, then cook for a further 30 minutes, or until reduced to a nice saucy consistency. Finely chop **6 sprigs of fresh flat-leaf parsley**, stir into the pan, season to perfection, and finish with a drizzle of **cold-pressed extra virgin olive oil**.

BORLOTTI BEANS

SERVES 6-8 | 2 HOURS, PLUS SOAKING

In a large casserole pan, cover **500g of dried borlotti beans** by 6cm with cold water and soak overnight. The next day, put the pan on a medium-low heat. Peel and add **6 whole cloves of garlic**, **1 potato** and **2 tablespoons of sun-dried tomato purée**. Cover and simmer for 1 to 2 hours, or until tender, stirring occasionally and adding splashes of water, if needed. Remove the potato and garlic, mash, and stir back through, then season to perfection. Uncovered, reduce to your desired consistency. Gently fry **10 fresh sage leaves** in a little **olive oil** until crispy, then spoon both leaves and oil over the beans, to serve.

PUY LENTILS

SERVES 8 | 25 MINUTES

Rinse **500g of Puy lentils**, place in a pan, cover with cold water, bring to the boil, then simmer for 20 minutes, or until tender. Meanwhile, finely slice a **100g piece of guanciale or smoked pancetta** and place in a large cold frying pan. Put it on a medium heat so the fat renders out, while you peel, finely slice and add **1 onion** and **2 cloves of garlic**. Cook for 15 minutes, stirring regularly. Add **8 tablespoons of balsamic vinegar** and cook until sticky and sweet. Drain and stir in the lentils, toss over the heat for 2 minutes, then season to perfection. Trim, very finely slice and toss through **1 radicchio**, to serve.

BRAISED GREENS

SERVES 4–6 | 20 MINUTES

Wash and trim **500g of mixed greens** (kale, cavolo nero, spinach, nettles, chard, rocket, herbs), removing tough stalks and finely slicing tender ones. Peel and finely slice **4 cloves of garlic** and place in a large casserole pan on a medium-high heat with **2 tablespoons of olive oil**, **1 small knob of unsalted butter** and **1 good pinch of dried red chilli flakes**. Stir until golden, then stir in any sliced tender stalks for 3 minutes. Tear in the thicker greens, followed 3 minutes later by the delicate ones. Cook on a low heat for another 3 minutes, season to perfection, then finish with a dribble of **white wine vinegar**.

THE MARKET NONNAS

SAN GIOVANNI DI DIO | ROME

Cooking with these wonderful women – two Nonna Marias, Nonna Lida, and lots of other lovely ladies I lost count of in the absolute chaos of the market – was as nuts as the place itself. It became a competition about how long everyone's been cooking for and what techniques to use, which just goes to show what an emotional subject food is. Everyone has their own nuances and ways of doing things! One thing's for sure, they all made very tasty food and shared with us lots of knowledge and inspiration.

BEAUTIFUL COURGETTES

GUANCIALE, PARSLEY & SWEET TOMATOES

〜〜〜〜〜〜〜〜〜〜〜〜

I enjoyed a taste of this colourful bowlful at the old fruit and veg market on the outskirts of Rome. It's a hectic place, but boy is everyone friendly. What I love is how such a simple combo of good ingredients really allows each one to sing. It's cheap, tasty, honest food, and the result is super-versatile, meaning it can be enjoyed as a side dish, an antipasto, tossed through pasta, piled on bruschetta, or even baked in a frittata.

SERVES 4-8 | 30-55 MINUTES

olive oil

1 clove of garlic

50g piece of guanciale (cured pig's cheek) or smoked pancetta

4 firm courgettes

200g ripe cherry tomatoes, on the vine

4 sprigs of fresh flat-leaf parsley

Place a large frying pan on a high heat with 1 tablespoon of oil. Peel and lightly squash the garlic clove and add to the pan, moving it around to perfume the oil. Slice the guanciale into rough 1cm chunks and add to the pan to let the fat render out. Trim the courgettes, halve lengthways, then chop into 2cm chunks. Stir into the pan, then season with a little sea salt and a good pinch of black pepper. Halve or quarter the tomatoes, deseed, and add to the pan. Pick, roughly chop and add the parsley leaves.

Reduce the heat to medium and cook for about 15 minutes, or until softened, stirring occasionally. This gives you a really fresh, delicious courgette dish full of life, just how Nonna Maria made it. Or you can turn the heat down lower and cook it for 40 minutes, so you get a deeper, sweeter, frumpier result, adding a splash of water to loosen, if needed. Both ways are delicious, and celebrate courgettes at their very best. Just before serving, taste and check you've got the seasoning spot on.

CALORIES	FAT	SAT FAT	PROTEIN	CARBS	SUGAR	SALT	FIBRE
122kcal	8.3g	2.2g	6.5g	5.6g	5.3g	0.7g	0.7g

ROMAN ARTICHOKES

STUFFED WITH HERBY GARLIC BREADCRUMBS & COOKED IN WHITE WINE

Carciofi alla Romana is a classic Italian artichoke dish with a wide use and appeal. These beauties are as at home served with grilled meat or fish as they are torn on a crostini with mozzarella as an antipasto, or even used in a primo risotto. The method is interesting because you fry and colour the artichokes, then add wine, which steams and tenderizes as it cooks away and the artichokes start to fry again, giving fantastic results.

SERVES 6-12 | 1 HOUR 30 MINUTES

12 large Italian violet
    artichokes

2 lemons, for artichoke prep

1 bulb of garlic

1 bunch of fresh flat-leaf
    parsley (30g)

6 anchovy fillets in oil

1 bunch of fresh mint (30g)

1 lemon

1 thick slice of stale rustic
    bread

extra virgin olive oil

olive oil

300ml Frascati white wine

8 mixed-colour olives
    (stone in)

First prep the artichokes (see page 382). When you're done, peel and chop the garlic and place in a food processor with the parsley (stalks and all) and anchovies. Pick in the mint leaves, finely grate in the lemon zest, tear in the bread, add 1 tablespoon of extra virgin olive oil and a pinch of sea salt and black pepper, then blitz until fine (or chop by hand, if you prefer).

Divide the mixture and stuff into the middle of each artichoke, really packing it in well. Place a deep, sturdy pan on a medium heat with 4 tablespoons of olive oil, then add the artichokes stuffed side down. Fry until lightly golden, trying not to touch or move the artichokes too much – just use one to check the colour. Pour in the wine to break the frying. Destone and throw in the olives, then cover with a scrunched-up sheet of wet greaseproof paper, pop the lid on ajar and cook for 20 minutes.

Remove the lid and paper, gently push the artichokes down to increase their surface area, then reduce to a low heat and leave until the wine has evaporated and the artichokes begin to fry again, becoming golden and crisp. Carefully remove to a warm platter, sprinkling any stuffing from the pan over the top. I like to add a splash of water and olive oil to the pan to scrape up any sticky bits, spoon that over the artichokes, then serve.

CALORIES	FAT	SAT FAT	PROTEIN	CARBS	SUGAR	SALT	FIBRE
243kcal	12.5g	2g	13.8g	17g	6g	1.3g	0.8g

BREAD & PASTRY

STUFFED FOCACCIA

BROAD BEANS, LEMON, PECORINO & FRESH HERBS

To this day, focaccia is still one of my favourite breads to bake. By stuffing it we get more texture, more layers, more contrast between soft and spongy, crisp and crunchy, and we celebrate seasonal broad beans.

SERVES 12 | 1 HOUR, PLUS PROVING

500g strong bread flour, plus extra for dusting

1 x 7g sachet of dried yeast

olive oil

750g broad beans, in their pods

4 cloves of garlic

1 bunch of fresh flat-leaf parsley (30g)

extra virgin olive oil

50g pecorino or Parmesan cheese

1 lemon

30g fine stale breadcrumbs

Put the flour and 5g of sea salt into a large bowl and make a well in the middle. In a jug, mix the yeast into 300ml of lukewarm water, leave for a few minutes, then gradually pour it into the well, stirring and bringing in the flour from the outside to form a dough. Knead on a flour-dusted surface for 10 minutes, or until smooth and springy. Place the dough in a lightly oiled bowl, cover with a clean damp tea towel and prove in a warm place for 1 hour, or until doubled in size. Meanwhile, pod the broad beans into a bowl, pinching the skins off any larger ones. Peel the garlic, finely chop with the top leafy half of the parsley and add to the bowl with 75ml of extra virgin olive oil. Finely grate in the pecorino and lemon zest, squeeze in the juice, season, mix together, then put aside.

Lightly oil a deep baking tray (30cm x 40cm), and dust evenly with the breadcrumbs. Pound the dough a few times with your fist, then roll or stretch it out to 30cm x 80cm. Drape half the dough into the tray, leaving the rest overhanging. Pour over the broad bean mixture in an even layer, keeping some of the oil behind. Fold the overhanging dough over the top, drizzle with the reserved oil, then use your fingers to gently push down and, importantly, create lots of dips and wells in the dough. Cover with a clean damp tea towel and leave to prove until doubled in size again.

Preheat the oven to 220°C. Sprinkle the dough with sea salt, then bake for 25 minutes, or until golden and cooked through. Let it cool on a board, then slice up and tuck in. Absolute heaven.

CALORIES	FAT	SAT FAT	PROTEIN	CARBS	SUGAR	SALT	FIBRE
256kcal	8.4g	1.9g	9.9g	37.5g	1.6g	1g	5.3g

PAGNOTTA

A CRUSTY, ROBUST, DELICIOUS SEMOLINA BREAD

Pagnotta – with its thick crust and spongy inside – is a typical daily bread in Italy. I've developed this recipe to ensure it's fun, easy and reliable for home baking. It does require an investment in time, but only when it comes to proving, and it's worth it – this bread really is a joy. The colour and flavour you get from using semolina flour is fantastic, and this bread is wonderful for all uses, whether fresh, toasted, or even stale.

MAKES 1 LARGE LOAF | 1 HOUR 10 MINUTES, PLUS PROVING OVERNIGHT

500g fine semolina flour, plus extra for dusting

500g strong white bread flour, plus extra for dusting

1 x 7g sachet of dried yeast

Place both flours and the yeast into the bowl of a free-standing mixer. Add 20g of sea salt and 750ml of lukewarm water, then beat slowly with the dough hook for 10 minutes, stopping occasionally to scrape down the sides with a rubber spatula – the mixture will still be very wet. Remove the dough hook, cover the bowl with a clean damp tea towel and leave to prove at room temperature in a draught-free spot overnight (at least 16 hours).

The next day, the dough will still be wet, but you should just be able to handle it. On a clean surface generously dusted with white bread flour, roughly shape the dough into a round, then carefully lift it into a floured metal bowl. Cover again with a clean damp tea towel and leave to prove somewhere warm (but not hot) for 3 hours, or until nearly doubled in size.

For the best results, place a large, heavy, lidded casserole pot in the oven (or you can use a high-sided pan), then preheat the oven to full whack (240°C). Gently turn out the dough on to a sheet of semolina-flour-dusted greaseproof paper. Generously sprinkle and rub the top of the dough with semolina flour, then slash the top with a sharp knife to help it swell and expand as it cooks. With a friend to help you, lift all four corners of the paper and carefully place the paper and dough in the hot pot. Cover and bake for 20 minutes. Remove the lid and bake for another 25 to 30 minutes, or until the bread is golden, risen, and the base sounds hollow when tapped. Transfer to a wire rack to cool before slicing.

THESE VALUES ARE BASED ON 1 SLICE

CALORIES	FAT	SAT FAT	PROTEIN	CARBS	SUGAR	SALT	FIBRE
195kcal	0.8g	0.2g	6.4g	43.2g	0.6g	1.1g	1.6g

NEAPOLITAN PIZZA BASE

CRISP, THIN, FLUFFY & DELICATE

Based on a lot of research, this is my take on a classic Neapolitan pizza base, and it's really reliable at home. The method might seem a bit back to front, but Neapolitans start with the liquid, then add the dry ingredients. Using a pizza stone in a conventional oven gives fantastic results, but a wood oven is the real holy grail.

MAKES 6 PIZZA BASES | 45 MINUTES, PLUS PROVING

1kg Tipo 00 flour, plus
   extra for dusting

1 x 7g sachet of dried yeast

olive oil

Pour 700ml of lukewarm water into a large bowl with 10g of sea salt. Gradually mix in a small handful of the flour to break the water and start to turn it into a batter. Mix in the yeast and leave for 2 minutes. Gradually mix in 90% of the remaining flour until you have a pliable, soft dough. Tip the remaining flour on to a clean surface and knead the dough for 20 minutes, or until smooth and elastic (or 10 minutes in a free-standing mixer with a dough hook). Place in a floured bowl, cover with a clean damp tea towel and prove for 1 hour, or until doubled in size. Knock out the air with your fists, roll into a sausage shape, chop into 6 equal pieces and roll each one into a ball, stretching the edges underneath. Place on an oiled tray, drizzle with oil, cover with clingfilm and the tea towel and prove overnight in the fridge (for better flavour and a more relaxed dough).

Preheat the oven to full whack (240°C) and place a pizza stone inside. Use a fish slice to move one ball of dough on to a flour-dusted surface. Press the ball out into a fat round disc, then pick it up and gently turn and stretch it to 30cm in diameter, using gravity to help you. Stretch it over the back of your fists, then place on a floured pizza paddle or board – the dough should be a little thicker around the edges. Pull it into shape and give it a jiggle so you know it's free-moving. Working quickly and with restraint, add your chosen toppings (see my favourites over the page). Quickly shunt on to your pizza stone and close the oven door to retain heat. Wait 7 or 8 minutes and it'll be golden, crisp and ready to eat.

CALORIES	FAT	SAT FAT	PROTEIN	CARBS	SUGAR	SALT	FIBRE
569kcal	2.6g	0.1g	23.8g	112.7g	2.6g	1.7g	4.3g

CLASSIC MARGHERITA

The Neapolitans don't mess around – they keep their tomato sauce beautifully simple, raw and fresh, so buying quality tinned tomatoes is a must. Simply scrunch **tinned San Marzano plum tomatoes** in your clean hands until smooth, then spoon over your pizza base. Top with a few **fresh basil leaves**, some torn **mozzarella cheese** and finely grated **Parmesan cheese**. Drizzle with a little **olive oil**, bake, and finish with a few extra basil leaves.

Spoon over **tomato sauce** (see recipe, left), then top with **ricotta cheese** mashed with **fresh marjoram leaves** and finely grated **Parmesan or pecorino cheese** and **lemon zest**. Add **baby courgettes** tossed in **olive oil** and **lemon juice**, drizzle with a little more **olive oil**, and bake.

Toss **red and black grapes**, **fresh rosemary leaves** and very finely sliced **red onion** in olive oil, then scatter over your pizza base with **pine nuts**, finely grated **pecorino cheese**, torn **mozzarella chesse** and a tiny drizzle of **runny honey**. Drizzle with a little **olive oil** and bake.

Spoon **tomato sauce** over your pizza base (see recipe, left), then scatter over some **fresh rosemary leaves** tossed with a little **olive oil**. Tear over some **spicy 'nduja**, finely grate over some **Parmesan cheese**, drizzle with a little more **olive oil**, and bake.

Spoon **tomato sauce** over your pizza base (see recipe, left), then top with small blanched **broccoli florets** fried with **garlic**, **fresh chilli**, **black olives (destoned)** and **sausagemeat**. Tear over some **provolone cheese**, drizzle with a little **olive oil**, and bake.

NONNA FERNANDA

OLD SPANISH QUARTER | NAPLES

Nonna Fernanda is a local legend. Born and raised in the neighbourhood, she's been cooking pizza fritta – the ultimate in street food and the original pizza – on the same spot since childhood. I'm sure it's her wonderfully feisty Neapolitan attitude that's kept her business – which her family set up more than a century ago – going all this time, and coupled with that, she has a real heart of gold. Her regulars just keep coming back for more.

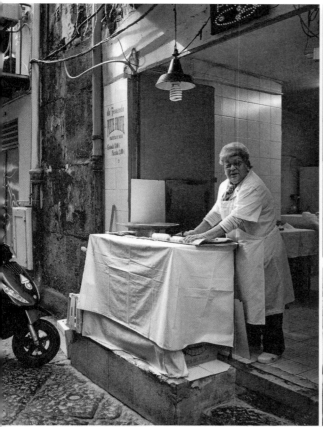

PIZZA FRITTA

STUFFED WITH RICOTTA, PARMESAN, MOZZARELLA & BASIL

Pizza fritta is one of the oldest forms of pizza, the classic street food of Naples, where it was easier to cook more using oil than managing a wood oven. The texture is almost doughnut-like on the outside, and creamy in the middle. Tweak this simple filling by adding any of your favourite ingredients to gently melt inside.

MAKES 12 | 1 HOUR

1 x Neapolitan pizza base recipe (see page 300)

1 x Hero tomato sauce (see page 372)

Tipo 00 flour, for dusting

100g Parmesan cheese

500g quality ricotta cheese

400g mozzarella cheese

1 bunch of fresh basil (30g)

2 litres vegetable oil, for frying

Make your dough (see page 300), proving it for 1 hour, rather than overnight, and your Hero tomato sauce (see page 372). When the time's up, divide the dough into 12 balls on a flour-dusted surface, dust them with flour, cover with a clean damp tea towel, and rest for 10 minutes.

One at a time, press out a ball of dough with your fingers, stretching and flattening it into a 15cm round. Finely grate the Parmesan and beat with the ricotta, then add a heaped spoonful to your dough round. Tear over a little mozzarella, season, push a few basil leaves into the top, then fold over the dough to seal the filling inside. Press down to stick, twisting and tucking the dough, if needed, like pizza ravioli! Repeat.

Heat the vegetable oil in a large, sturdy pan over a medium-high heat. Drop in a cube of potato and when it's golden and rises to the surface, the oil is ready. I'm not a lover of deep-frying but it does give the best results here – please be careful. Working in batches, lower in two fritte to cook for 1½ minutes on each side, or until golden. Remove to a plate lined with kitchen paper to drain, then let the oil come back up to temperature before adding the next two. Warm the tomato sauce and serve on the side for dunking. Sprinkle more fresh basil leaves over the fritte, to serve.

CALORIES	FAT	SAT FAT	PROTEIN	CARBS	SUGAR	SALT	FIBRE
640kcal	32.4g	11.2g	26.3g	60.9g	5.1g	1.7g	2.9g

FOCACCIA

SPIKED WITH PORK CRACKLINGS, OREGANO, SEA SALT & WALNUTS

Focaccia can be made to fill a whole tray, or shaped into a round like this one. I love the way you can change and embellish the toppings based on what's in season or available – here we're celebrating walnuts and oregano, as well as crunchy salty pork cracklings, taking the already mighty focaccia to a whole new level.

SERVES 12 | 1 HOUR, PLUS PROVING

1 x 7g sachet of dried yeast

1 bunch of fresh oregano (30g)

50g pork fat (ask your butcher)

500g strong bread flour, plus extra for dusting

olive oil

50g pork skin (ask your butcher)

30g fine stale breadcrumbs

25g shelled walnut halves

Preheat the oven to 220°C. In a jug, mix the yeast into 300ml of lukewarm water. Strip half the oregano leaves into a food processor, add the pork fat and blitz until fine. Add the flour, 5g of sea salt and the bubbly yeast mixture, and blitz again until it just comes together into a ball of dough. Knead on a flour-dusted surface for 5 minutes, or until smooth and springy. Place in a lightly oiled bowl, cover with a clean damp tea towel and prove in a warm place for 1 hour, or until doubled in size. Meanwhile, place the pork skin on a large baking tray and roast for 30 minutes, or until golden and puffed up. Remove the crackling to a plate, then sprinkle the breadcrumbs over the fat on the tray and leave to cool.

When ready, pound the dough a few times with your fist, then stretch it out into a large round about 2cm thick. Arrange the breadcrumbs on the tray into a circle the same size as the dough, then place it on top. Push down roughly with your fingers to create dips and wells. Snap the crackling into small pieces and scatter over, pushing them into the surface. Cover again and prove for another hour, until the dough has doubled in size.

Bake the bread for 25 to 30 minutes, or until dark golden and cooked through. Crumble up the walnuts and, with the remaining oregano leaves, dress with a little oil, then scatter over the top. Sprinkle with a pinch of sea salt from a height. Return to the oven for 5 more minutes, then remove and leave to cool before slicing and serving.

CALORIES	FAT	SAT FAT	PROTEIN	CARBS	SUGAR	SALT	FIBRE
209kcal	6.3g	1.7g	7.4g	32.7g	0.7g	0.6g	1.6g

WILD GREENS TORTA

OLIVE OIL PASTRY, SULTANAS, OLIVES & PINE NUTS

You'd typically get a slice of this delicious filled pastry as an antipasto, though it also makes a delightful lunch, and is very good served cold the following day. Cooking the wild greens down until dark and dense gives the most incredible depth of flavour, which works beautifully with the sweetness from the sultanas and onions, and the saltiness from the olives and anchovies. Choose your greens to reflect the season.

SERVES 10–12 | 1 HOUR 40 MINUTES

½ x Olive oil pastry
  (see page 380)

6 cloves of garlic

6 anchovy fillets in oil

olive oil

¾ teaspoon dried red chilli
  flakes

2 red onions

1.2kg mixed wild green leaves,
  such as spinach, chard,
  rocket, herbs, stinging
  nettles

50g olives (stone in)

75g sultanas or currants

75g pine nuts

50g Parmesan cheese

1 large egg

Start by making the Olive oil pastry (see page 380). To make the filling, peel the garlic and finely slice with the anchovies, then place in a large, deep pan on a medium heat with 6 tablespoons of oil and the chilli flakes. Stir occasionally while you peel and finely slice the onions, then stir them into the pan. Continue to stir while you pick through the greens, discarding any tough stalks (trimmed chard stalks can be finely chopped and added to the pan). Wash the greens well and roughly chop them.

Squash and destone the olives, tearing the flesh into the pan. Add the greens, in batches, then the sultanas and pine nuts. Cook down for 25 minutes, or until dark, intense and the excess moisture has cooked away, stirring regularly. Finely grate in the Parmesan, taste and check the seasoning, then leave to cool. Preheat the oven to 180°C.

Roll out half the pastry into a 30cm round, about 3mm thick, then loosely roll it up around the rolling pin. Unroll it over a 23cm non-stick loose-bottomed sandwich tin, easing it into the sides and edges. Tip in the filling in an even layer, then roll out the remaining pastry and place on top, trimming and pinching it to fit. Re-roll any offcuts to make a lattice pattern on the top, if you like, using beaten egg to stick the extra pieces in place. Eggwash the top, then bake at the bottom of the oven for 1 hour, or until beautifully golden. Leave to cool a little, then release, slice and serve.

CALORIES	FAT	SAT FAT	PROTEIN	CARBS	SUGAR	SALT	FIBRE
557kcal	33.8g	5.4g	16.6g	47.6g	9.6g	1.2g	3.2g

TARALLI

CRISPY, CRUNCHY, MINI ITALIAN BAGELS WITH FENNEL & SALT

~~~~~~

Taralli biscuits are commonly found in the south, and enjoyed as a snack or part of an antipasti spread. I love the way some people rehydrate them in water to make them soft again, then serve them with really beautiful, simple toppings. I had a bit of fun with that over the page, and I hope you have fun with them, too.

MAKES 12 | 1 HOUR 20 MINUTES, PLUS PROVING & COOLING

½ x 7g sachet of dried yeast

1 tablespoon fennel seeds

300g Tipo 00 flour, plus
    extra for dusting

300g fine semolina flour

125ml Prosecco

extra virgin olive oil

white wine vinegar

In a jug, cover the yeast with 125ml of lukewarm water. Bash the fennel seeds, 1 level teaspoon of sea salt and a good pinch of black pepper in a pestle and mortar until fine, then tip into a large bowl with both flours. Stir in the yeast mixture, Prosecco and 100ml of oil. Knead on a flour-dusted surface until smooth and springy. Return to the bowl, cover with a clean damp tea towel and leave to prove in a warm place for 1 hour.

When the time's up, divide the dough into 12 equal-sized balls, then roll each into an 18cm-long sausage. Fold each one around and over itself into a ring, pressing and sticking the ends together with a little water. Prove on a tray lined with greaseproof paper for 30 minutes.

Preheat the oven to 180°C. In batches, poach the taralli for 10 minutes in a pan of boiling water, turning halfway, then remove to a tea towel to dry. Place on two trays lined with greaseproof paper and bake for 30 to 35 minutes, or until golden, swapping the trays around halfway.

Once cool enough to handle, you can tuck in as is or, if you want to have fun with it, slice the taralli in half and leave them to dry out on wire racks in the sun or in an oven on a low temperature. When you want to eat, refresh the taralli: add a good pinch of salt and 1 tablespoon each of oil and vinegar to a large bowl of water. Plop in the taralli, soak for 1 minute, then drain on a wire rack. Now get topping! See over for inspiration . . .

CALORIES	FAT	SAT FAT	PROTEIN	CARBS	SUGAR	SALT	FIBRE
257kcal	9.2g	1.2g	6.3g	36.9g	1.1g	0.5g	1.4g

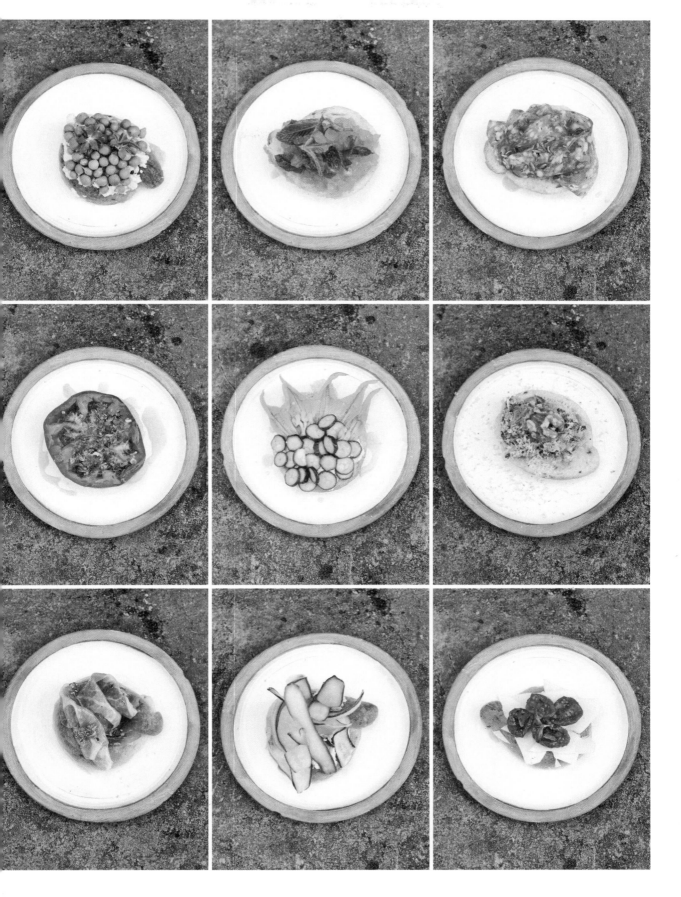

MOZZARELLA BREAD

SMOKY SCAMORZA, SMASHED GREEN OLIVES, CAPERS & OREGANO

~~~~~~

Everything about this wonderful Italian bread makes me happy – it's ridiculously delicious. The fragrance of the olives and capers really sings out, and teamed with good seasoning and the incredible ooze of the cheeses, debatably this is even more wonderful than a pizza. Make this bread, and it won't hang around for long.

SERVES 12 | 1 HOUR 15 MINUTES, PLUS PROVING

4 tablespoons baby capers in brine

500g strong bread flour, plus extra for dusting

1 x 7g sachet of dried yeast

olive oil

250g large green olives (stone in)

1 big bunch of fresh oregano or thyme (60g), ideally the flowering kind

60g Parmesan cheese

extra virgin olive oil

2 tablespoons white wine vinegar

2 x 125g balls of buffalo mozzarella cheese

200g scamorza (smoked mozzarella cheese)

Soak the capers in a bowl of water. Put the flour and 5g of sea salt into a large bowl and make a well in the middle. In a jug, mix the yeast into 300ml of lukewarm water, then gradually pour it into the well, stirring and bringing in the flour from the outside to form a dough. Knead on a flour-dusted surface for 10 minutes, or until smooth and springy. Place in a lightly oiled bowl, cover with a clean damp tea towel and prove in a warm place for 2 hours, or until doubled in size. Meanwhile, destone the olives, then pound with the drained capers, half the oregano leaves and a pinch of sea salt in a pestle and mortar until you have a rough paste. Finely grate in the Parmesan, add a couple of pinches of black pepper, then muddle in 6 tablespoons of extra virgin olive oil and the vinegar.

On a flour-dusted surface, pull or roll the dough out to a rectangle about 30cm x 60cm. Spread the smashed-up olive mixture all over the dough, then randomly tear over the mozzarella and scamorza. Starting from one of the longest sides, roll it up into a giant sausage. Lightly oil a large baking dish or ovenproof pan and dust with a little flour, then either use your hands to squeeze and tear the dough or cut it into rough 5cm pieces, placing them swirl side up in the pan. Poke the remaining oregano sprigs in and around, then drizzle with a little olive oil. Leave to prove for 1 hour, or until doubled in size. Preheat the oven to 200°C.

Gently place the dish in the middle of the oven for 30 minutes, or until the bread is golden. Leave to rest for at least 15 minutes before tucking in.

CALORIES	FAT	SAT FAT	PROTEIN	CARBS	SUGAR	SALT	FIBRE
345kcal	18.1g	5.1g	14.4g	31.7g	0.9g	1.5g	1.3g

NONNA TITTA

PROCIDA | NAPLES

Nonna Titta is known on the island as one of the best cooks of traditional Procidan cuisine – if there are local celebrations or festivities, you can be sure she'll be cooking up a storm. Titta has a big family, and is used to feeding a crowd. The carnival lasagne recipe she shared with me, which she learnt from her grandmother, is absolutely epic and a firm family favourite, and I can see why! Make it yourself from the pages that follow.

CARNIVAL LASAGNE

BAKED LAYERS OF TOMATO & RICOTTA SPAGHETTI & MEATBALLS

Made for sharing, this is a very flamboyant, fun and incredibly delicious type of lasagne. It's perfect for a party or a big weekend feast with friends, and guaranteed to make everyone smile from ear to ear.

SERVES 12 | 2 HOURS

¼ x Olive oil pastry
  (see page 380)

1kg dried spaghetti

4 cloves of garlic

2 fresh red chillies

olive oil

500g mixed minced beef
  & pork

5 large eggs

50g coarse stale breadcrumbs

1 bunch of fresh basil (30g)

150ml Greco di Tufo white
  wine

3 x 400g tins of quality
  plum tomatoes

100g Parmesan cheese

250g ricotta cheese

10 slices of prosciutto

Make your Olive oil pastry (see page 380). Cook the pasta in a large pan of boiling salted water for 2 minutes less than the packet instructions, then drain well. Meanwhile, peel the garlic, finely slice with the chillies, and place both in a large frying pan on a medium heat with 1 tablespoon of oil. Fry for 2 minutes, while you scrunch the meat with 1 egg, the breadcrumbs and a pinch of sea salt and black pepper. Roll into 2cm balls, adding them to the pan as you go. Cook for 5 minutes, tossing until lightly golden all over. Tear in 20 basil leaves. Pour in the wine and let it cook away. Scrunch in the tomatoes through clean hands, then pour in 1 tin's worth of water. Simmer for 5 minutes, taste, and season to perfection.

Preheat the oven to 180°C. Finely grate half the Parmesan over the drained pasta, add the remaining 4 eggs and 2 tablespoons of oil, toss well, then divide between two bowls. Mix the ricotta into the first bowl. Removing the meatballs to one side, toss the tomato sauce into the second bowl, loosening with a splash of water, if needed.

Now for the good bit – the layering. Place half the tomato pasta in a deep 30cm baking dish. Pick over a few basil leaves, finely grate over a little Parmesan, and lay over half the prosciutto. Arrange half the ricotta pasta on top, then the meatballs. Repeat the ricotta pasta layer, add the rest of the basil, Parmesan and prosciutto, and finish with the remaining tomato pasta. Roll out the pastry to 3mm thick, cut into strips and arrange over the pasta, as creatively as you like. Bake at the bottom of the oven for 40 minutes, or until golden. Slice and serve right away.

CALORIES	FAT	SAT FAT	PROTEIN	CARBS	SUGAR	SALT	FIBRE
683kcal	26g	8g	33.2g	82g	6.8g	1g	3.8g

ICE-CREAM SANDWICHES

SICILIAN STYLE WITH BERRIES, NUTS & MELTED CHOCOLATE

Mastering a soft, spongy, delicate brioche bun is a good technique to have up your sleeve. You can, of course, leave out the sugar and make these buns for burgers or sandwiches, but here, served hot with melting ice cream, gooey chocolate, berries and other bits – what can I say, it's an absolute treat. Very naughty, very nice.

SERVES 12 | 50 MINUTES, PLUS PROVING

150ml whole milk

½ x 7g sachet of dried yeast

300g strong bread flour,
  plus extra for dusting

200g Tipo 00 flour

60g golden caster sugar

60g unsalted butter (cold),
  plus extra for brushing

2 large eggs

olive oil

icing sugar, for dusting

FILLINGS

ice cream, chocolate, cream,
  seasonal berries, your
  favourite nuts – get creative!

Pour the milk into a pan with 75ml of water and heat until just warm. Stir in the yeast and put aside. Sieve the flours into a large mixing bowl with the sugar and 10g of sea salt. Cube the butter and rub into the dry mixture with your fingertips until it resembles crumbs. Pour in the milk, crack in the eggs, and mix with your fingers into a loose sticky dough, moving it for 4 minutes until shiny. It's a wet dough, but it will come together! Tip it on to a clean surface, pick it up and throw it down, then repeat about 40 times. Some dough will stick, but just scrape it back up as you go. You should end up with a smooth, elastic dough that comes off the surface and your hands easily. Place in an oiled bowl, cover with a clean damp tea towel and leave at room temperature for 2 hours, or until doubled in size.

Tip the dough on to a flour-dusted surface and divide into 12 equal pieces. Shape into balls, then roll into little fat rounds or cigars and place on baking trays lined with greaseproof paper. Cover and leave to rise for 2 hours. Preheat the oven to 180°C. Bake for 15 to 20 minutes, or until golden. Brush with melted butter, then transfer to a wire rack.

Now the fun bit – the fillings! Get yourself a few different tubs of ice cream – vanilla, strawberry, chocolate, salted caramel, lemon, you name it. Toast and bash or chop nuts to create different textures. Line up a bowl of chocolate sauce and whipped cream, plus some seasonal berries, and go to town. Dust with icing sugar, and devour.

CALORIES	FAT	SAT FAT	PROTEIN	CARBS	SUGAR	SALT	FIBRE
220kcal	6.1g	3.3g	6.9g	36g	6.5g	0.9g	1.3g

DESSERT

CHOCOLATE CANNOLI
CRUNCHY PASTA TUBES STUFFED WITH SILKY CHOCOLATE GRAPPA RICOTTA

Cannoli are fantastic. Traditionally they're bigger than mine and contain chunks of candied fruit, nuts and chocolate, but I wanted to go a bit more delicate, and ricotta is the filling hero here. It is helpful to buy some metal cannoli tubes, which you can get online – just squeeze them to 2cm in diameter before use.

MAKES 24 | 1 HOUR 30 MINUTES, PLUS RESTING

2 large eggs

60ml sweet wine or Marsala

olive oil

250g plain or Tipo 00 flour, plus extra for dusting

1 litre sunflower oil, for frying

200g dark chocolate (70%)

100g toasted hazelnuts

600g quality ricotta cheese

1 teaspoon vanilla bean paste

2 tablespoons runny honey

2 heaped teaspoons quality cocoa powder

1 tablespoon grappa

In a large bowl, whip 1 egg with the sweet wine and 3 tablespoons of oil. Gradually add the flour (you may not need it all) until it comes together into a ball of dough. Knead for a few minutes, or until smooth and silky. Wrap in clingfilm and leave to rest for 1 hour.

Pour the sunflower oil into a large, sturdy pan on a medium-high heat, and leave it to get to 180°C on a thermometer. Meanwhile, roll the dough into a large sausage about 4cm in diameter. Keeping the rest of the dough covered with a clean damp tea towel, slice off a ½cm-thick disc and roll into a ball, then flatten out on a flour-dusted surface to 2mm thick. Lightly dust your metal cannoli tubes with flour (or use lightly oiled dried cannelloni tubes), then wrap a circle of dough around each, sealing the edges with beaten egg. Working in batches, carefully lower into the hot oil for just 1 minute, to get lightly golden. Remove to a plate lined with kitchen paper to drain for 3 minutes, then squeeze the moulds and gently slide off the cannoli. Repeat until you've used up all the dough.

Melt the chocolate. Pound the hazelnuts in a pestle and mortar until fine. Drain the ricotta, then blitz in a food processor with the vanilla paste, honey, cocoa and grappa until just smooth. Spoon into a piping bag with a star nozzle, and twist the bag to give tension, then pipe the filling into the cannoli. Drizzle with chocolate, sprinkle with nuts, and serve.

CALORIES	FAT	SAT FAT	PROTEIN	CARBS	SUGAR	SALT	FIBRE
192kcal	12.1g	4g	5.1g	15.9g	7.7g	0.1g	0.6g

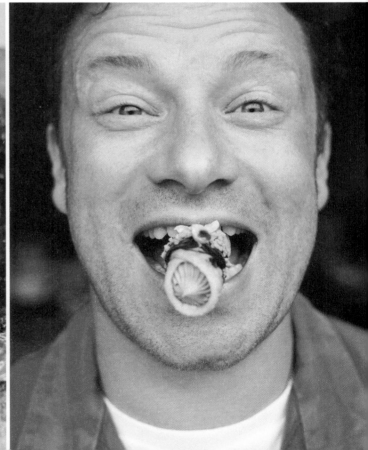

TUSCAN RICE TART

BAKED CUSTARD & SEASONAL FRUIT

~~~~~~

I've always loved rice pudding, and the best bit for me is that crispy skin you get when it's baked. That's kind of what this tart is all about – crispy top, sweet and sour fruit, rich, creamy rice and custard. Pudding heaven.

SERVES 8 | 1 HOUR 20 MINUTES

200g Arborio risotto rice

250ml semi-skimmed milk

250ml single cream

1 small pinch of saffron

1 cinnamon stick

2 vanilla pods

4 large eggs

100g caster sugar

unsalted butter, for greasing

3 ripe plums or pears

olive oil

Preheat the oven to 180°C. Cook the rice in a pan of boiling water for 10 minutes, then drain well. Meanwhile, for the custard, pour the milk and cream into a pan with the saffron and cinnamon. Split the vanilla pods lengthways and scrape out the seeds, adding both pods and seeds to the pan. Simmer on a medium heat for 5 minutes, then remove and leave to infuse for a few minutes. Discard the vanilla pods and cinnamon.

Separate the eggs (save the whites for another recipe). In a large bowl, whisk the yolks with 70g of the sugar until pale. Whisking constantly, ladle a little of the infused milk mixture on to the yolks. Continue to add the milk, a ladleful at a time, whisking each addition in well before adding the next. When you've mixed in all the milk, stir in the drained rice.

Grease and line a 23cm pie tin or baking dish. Sprinkle in 1 tablespoon of sugar, shaking gently to coat the base and sides. Pour in the custard mixture – the rice should sink to the bottom, giving two nice layers when it's baked. Prep your fruit, removing any stones or seeds and halving or slicing as appropriate, then toss with 1 tablespoon of oil and the remaining sugar. Gently arrange the fruit on top of the custard. Bake for 50 minutes, or until dark golden and set. Leave to cool to room temperature, then turn out, slice, and serve. This is also delicious enjoyed cold.

CALORIES	FAT	SAT FAT	PROTEIN	CARBS	SUGAR	SALT	FIBRE
257kcal	9.2g	3.8g	7g	38.2g	16.8g	0.2g	0.4g

AMALFI LEMON TART

WHITE WINE, OLIVE OIL & VANILLA PASTRY

This wonderful, rather delicious baked lemon tart is fresh but comforting and just a stone's throw away from a baked cheesecake. It's great served with ice cream, and really nice with seasonal berries, such as raspberries or strawberries. If you're feeling the Italian vibe, a little slice for breakfast with a black coffee is a real treat.

SERVES 10-12 | 2 HOURS, PLUS CHILLING

PASTRY

250g plain flour, plus extra
for dusting

50g icing sugar, plus extra
for dusting

75ml olive oil

75ml Greco di Tufo white
wine

½ teaspoon vanilla bean paste

FILLING

5 large lemons

500g quality ricotta cheese

150g caster sugar

2 large eggs

To make the pastry, put the flour and icing sugar into a large bowl with a good pinch of sea salt. Make a well in the middle, then add the oil, wine and vanilla paste. Use a fork to whip up the wet mixture, gradually bringing the flour in from the outside until it comes together as a ball of dough. Tip on to a lightly floured surface and knead for just a couple of minutes, then wrap in clingfilm and place in the fridge for 30 minutes.

On a flour-dusted surface, roll out the pastry to about 3mm thick. Loosely roll it up around the rolling pin and unroll it over a 25cm loose-bottomed tart tin, easing and pushing it carefully into the sides. Trim off any excess, patch up any holes, then prick the base with a fork, cover with clingfilm, and chill in the freezer for 1 hour 30 minutes.

Preheat the oven to 180°C. When the time's up, bake the pastry case blind for 25 minutes, or until lightly golden. Meanwhile, finely grate the zest of 1 lemon and put aside. Squeeze all the lemons to give you 150ml of juice, then whisk with the rest of the filling ingredients until smooth, by hand or in a food processor. Pour into the tart case and bake for 30 minutes, dusting with icing sugar and sprinkling over the lemon zest for the last 5 minutes. Transfer to a wire rack to cool – it will have a slight wobble, but will set as it cools. Dust with extra icing sugar, then slice and serve.

CALORIES	FAT	SAT FAT	PROTEIN	CARBS	SUGAR	SALT	FIBRE
323kcal	14.4g	4.9g	8.5g	41.5g	22.8g	0.2g	0.8g

BARONESSA SUSANNA

TURIN | PIEDMONT

Baronessa Susanna welcomed me into her home, where she was looking after and cooking with her grandchildren. We had the pleasure of cooking up some lovely dishes together, which demonstrated the lasting influence of the once French-ruled Turin. Her favourite dessert, which she has been cooking for years, is a kind of chocolaty crème caramel with a layer of biscuit that floats to the top as it cooks, becoming the base when you turn it out. It's wonderful. Make it yourself from the pages that follow.

COCOA RUM DESSERT

AMARETTI, CARAMEL & CRÈME FRAÎCHE

~~~~~~

Baronessa Susanna cooked this delightful dessert for me in Turin. The layers in texture from the crunchy amaretti biscuit base to the smooth, silky chocolate middle and the shiny caramel top create the most perfect mouthful – it feels wonderfully decadent. Plus rum, cocoa and caramel are a match made in heaven.

SERVES 10 | 1 HOUR 20 MINUTES, PLUS COOLING

unsalted butter, for greasing

100g caster sugar

50g brown sugar

4 large eggs

500ml whole milk

3 heaped tablespoons
   quality cocoa powder

50ml golden rum

200g amaretti biscuits

crème fraîche, to serve

Preheat the oven to 160°C, and grease a long 1.5-litre loaf tin with butter. Melt the caster sugar in a small non-stick frying pan on a medium-high heat until you get a rich, chestnutty caramel – swirl the pan to help the sugar melt, but don't touch or stir it. Carefully pour the caramel into the loaf tin and tilt it around until the base is evenly covered.

Whisk the brown sugar with the eggs for 3 minutes, or until light and slightly thickened. Whisk in the milk, cocoa and rum for 30 seconds, then crumble in and stir through the amaretti biscuits. Pour the mixture into the loaf tin. Half-fill a deep-sided roasting tray with hot tap water, and sit the loaf tin in the centre. Carefully transfer to the middle of the oven and bake for 1 hour. Remove and leave to cool in the tin, then pop into the fridge to chill for at least 4 hours, or until needed.

To serve, carefully run a knife around the edge of the tin, then gently turn out the dessert on to a serving board or platter, spooning over any caramel left behind in the tin. Serve each portion with a spoonful of crème fraîche.

CALORIES	FAT	SAT FAT	PROTEIN	CARBS	SUGAR	SALT	FIBRE
233kcal	9.2g	2.6g	7.8g	28.2g	27.4g	0.2g	1.6g

ZEPPOLE

PIPED PASTRY BUNS WITH CUSTARD & GIANDUJA

Traditionally these are deep-fried, but baking means the recipe is much more accessible at home and a tad less indulgent, too. My zeppole are super-fine, delicate, and the perfect handheld receptacle for tasty fillings.

MAKES 20 | 2 HOURS, PLUS COOLING

30g unsalted butter (cold)

100g Tipo 00 flour

40g fine semolina flour

3 large eggs

150g Gianduja (see page 348)

icing sugar, for dusting

CUSTARD

1 vanilla pod

600ml whole milk

4 large eggs

100g golden caster sugar

50g cornflour

Preheat the oven to 200°C. Place the butter in a medium pan with 250ml of cold water, and bring to the boil over a medium heat. Meanwhile, sieve the flour and semolina flour into a bowl with a pinch of sea salt. Beat the eggs in a separate bowl. As soon as the butter mixture comes to a rolling boil, tip in the flour mixture and, with a wooden spoon, carefully but quickly and fairly vigorously beat it together until smooth and starting to come away from the sides. Remove from the heat and gradually beat in the eggs. Transfer to a piping bag fitted with a 1cm star-shaped nozzle.

Line two baking sheets with greaseproof paper, using a little mix to stick the paper down at the corners, then pipe out 20 x 4cm swirls. Bake for 25 minutes, or until golden and crisp, swapping the trays halfway for even cooking. Turn the oven off, open the door and leave the zeppole to cool while you make the custard. Halve the vanilla pod and scrape out the seeds, then place both pod and seeds in a pan on a medium-low heat with the milk to gently infuse. Meanwhile, whisk the eggs and caster sugar in a large bowl until pale and fluffy, then whisk in the cornflour. When the milk is almost boiling, remove the vanilla pod, then slowly whisk the milk into the egg mixture. Pour it back into the pan and whisk until thickened. Pour the custard into a bowl (sieving if needed), then cover and chill in the fridge while you make the Gianduja (see page 348).

To serve, there are no rules – pipe, stuff or spoon in the Gianduja and custard (saving any leftovers). Dust with icing sugar. Nice with cherries.

CALORIES	FAT	SAT FAT	PROTEIN	CARBS	SUGAR	SALT	FIBRE
158kcal	8.3g	3g	4.8g	17.1g	9.9g	0.2g	0.3g

LIMONCELLO TIRAMISÙ

VANILLA MASCARPONE, CRUSHED CHERRIES & WHITE CHOCOLATE

Of course this is not a traditional tiramisù, but the layering of the sponge and silky vanilla mascarpone provides the link to the dessert we all know and love. Using cherries, limoncello and white chocolate gives you a lighter feeling dessert that is hugely enjoyable, inspired by long summer days along the Amalfi coast.

SERVES 8 | 45 MINUTES, PLUS CHILLING

2 oranges

200ml limoncello

4 tablespoons runny honey

200g sponge fingers

200ml good espresso (cold)

250g mascarpone cheese

250g natural yoghurt

1 teaspoon vanilla bean paste

250g ripe cherries

extra virgin olive oil

100g white chocolate (cold)

Use a speed-peeler to peel strips of zest from the oranges into a small pan. Squeeze over all the juice, add 100ml of the limoncello and 2 tablespoons of honey, and simmer over a medium heat until you have a thick syrup.

Cover the base of a 24cm serving bowl with half the sponge fingers (or you can use the sponge trimmings from my Amalfi rum baba recipe on page 352, giving you an excuse to make both!). Mix the cold espresso with the remaining limoncello, then drizzle half of it over the sponge layer, pressing down lightly to help it absorb the coffee mixture.

Whisk together the mascarpone, yoghurt, vanilla paste and remaining 2 tablespoons of honey until smooth, then spoon half into the bowl in an even layer. Remove the stones from the cherries, tearing the flesh over the mascarpone. Lay the remaining sponge fingers on top, drizzle over the rest of the coffee, and finish by spooning over the remaining mascarpone.

Spoon the syrup and candied peel over the tiramisù, and drizzle with a little extra virgin olive oil. Cover and pop into the fridge for at least 4 hours, or overnight. Shave or grate over the white chocolate to finish.

CALORIES	FAT	SAT FAT	PROTEIN	CARBS	SUGAR	SALT	FIBRE
443kcal	20.9g	12.7g	6.3g	44.9g	38.9g	0.2g	1g

APRICOT SORBET

MACERATED CHERRIES, AMARETTI & EDIBLE FLOWERS

Apricots are one of my favourite fruits, and they grow in abundance in Basilicata. When stewed simply with fig leaves, the flavours transport me straight back to southern Italy. If you can't get fig leaves, try using a little fresh basil or lemon verbena in their place to impart that extra flavour to the mixture as it cools. Beautiful.

SERVES 10 | 25 MINUTES, PLUS COOLING & FREEZING

150g caster sugar

1kg ripe apricots

optional: 8 fig leaves

1 x 600g jar of cherries in syrup

100g amaretti biscuits

optional: edible flowers

Put the sugar into a pan with 250ml of water, bring to the boil on a high heat, then let the sugar dissolve. Quarter and destone the apricots and add to the pan. Stir, cover, and simmer on a medium heat for 10 minutes, or until soft and tender. Turn the heat off, add the fig leaves to the pan (if using) and leave them to infuse the mixture as it cools down.

Once cool, remove the fig leaves, then blitz the mixture in a blender until smooth. Pour into a ceramic serving dish, cover, and freeze for 8 hours, forking up the mixture every hour to break down the ice crystals.

Remove the sorbet from the freezer around 15 minutes before you want to serve up. Decant the cherries into a nice serving dish, crush the amaretti biscuits into a fine dust in a pestle and mortar, or bash up with a rolling pin, and pick some small edible flowers (if using). Take it all to the table with your dish of sorbet, and serve up pretty little portions to order.

CALORIES	FAT	SAT FAT	PROTEIN	CARBS	SUGAR	SALT	FIBRE
177kcal	2.2g	0.2g	2.6g	39g	38.9g	0g	0.9g

CHOCOLATE CHICKPEA CAKE

SWEET ORANGE SYRUP

~~~~~~

In Basilicata, chickpeas are everywhere! I got quite excited about how you can use them almost like chestnuts in baking, and this hybrid of a cake and a brownie is the result. I love its simplicity – it's truly delicious.

SERVES 18 | 40 MINUTES, PLUS COOLING

150g unsalted butter

extra virgin olive oil

350g golden caster sugar

150g dark chocolate (70%)

1 x 400g tin of chickpeas

3 large eggs

150g plain flour

1 teaspoon baking powder

2 oranges

Preheat the oven to 170°C and line a baking tray (20cm x 30cm) with greaseproof paper. In a pan on a very low heat, melt the butter with 4 tablespoons of extra virgin olive oil and 250g of the sugar until combined, stirring with a rubber spatula. Snap in the chocolate, turn off the heat, and stir gently until the chocolate has melted and the mixture is smooth.

Drain the chickpeas, blitz well in a food processor, then pour in the chocolate mixture and blitz again until smooth. With the processor still running, add the eggs one by one. Pulse in the flour, baking powder and a pinch of sea salt until just combined, then pour the mixture evenly into the tray. Bake for 20 to 25 minutes, or until risen and springy to the touch.

Meanwhile, make your syrup. Use a speed-peeler to peel off strips of zest from both oranges into a small pan. Squeeze in all the juice, add the remaining 100g of sugar and simmer on a medium-low heat until you have a nice syrupy consistency – don't be tempted to touch it! Leave to cool.

As soon as your cake comes out of the oven, poke holes in it with a cocktail stick or fine skewer, then spoon over most of the cooled syrup so it soaks into the sponge. Arrange the peel on top to decorate. Leave to cool completely, then slice and serve. I like mine with a nice scoop of vanilla ice cream and a drizzle of the remaining syrup (plus a good cup of tea!).

CALORIES	FAT	SAT FAT	PROTEIN	CARBS	SUGAR	SALT	FIBRE
265kcal	13.2g	6.4g	3.6g	35.2g	26.4g	0.3g	0.8g

GIANDUJA

THE ORIGINAL NUTELLA

~~~~~~

As is often the case with beautiful recipes, the creation of gianduja was due to the austerity of restrictions placed on imports to Europe, meaning chocolate was in short supply. To stretch it further, chocolatier Michele Prochet blended his supplies with ground hazelnuts – genius. It couldn't be easier to make from scratch, plus you have a wonderful gift to share – your lucky, lucky recipients won't stop talking about it!

MAKES 600G | 15 MINUTES

150g blanched hazelnuts

400g dark chocolate (70%)

100g icing sugar

mild olive oil

Preheat the oven to 180°C. Toast the hazelnuts in a roasting tray for 6 minutes, or until lightly golden. Remove to a food processor and blitz to your desired consistency – I like a little bit of crunch but it's up to you whether to go smooth or chunky. Meanwhile, melt the chocolate in a heatproof bowl over a pan of gently simmering water, stirring occasionally. Once smooth, add a little pinch of sea salt, sift in the icing sugar, pour in 200ml of oil, sprinkle in the blitzed hazelnuts and stir to combine. Easy!

You can eat the gianduja right away, or keep it in a sterilized jar for up to 6 weeks in a cool, dark place. Once opened, use within a couple of weeks. Forgive me for stating the obvious, but it's delicious on toast, in or on croissants, drizzled over pancakes, layered between cake sponges, in my Zeppole (see page 340), or even tossed through fresh pasta.

THESE VALUES ARE BASED ON 50G

CALORIES	FAT	SAT FAT	PROTEIN	CARBS	SUGAR	SALT	FIBRE
306kcal	23.9g	6g	2.4g	21.6g	21.2g	0.1g	0.6g

AMALFI RUM BABA

SOAKED IN TUTTI-FRUTTI LIMONCELLO SYRUP

~~~~~~

I first made this extravagant drunken sponge dessert with Gennaro back when I was a teenager. I love the concept of rehydrating sponge with flavoured syrup to make it even more sumptuous and delicious. Enjoy.

SERVES 20 | 2 HOURS 50 MINUTES, PLUS PROVING & SOAKING OVERNIGHT

BABA

1 x 7g sachet of dried yeast

250g unsalted butter, plus extra for greasing

12 large eggs

750g self-raising flour, plus extra for dusting

SYRUP

500g golden caster sugar

750ml limoncello

1 vanilla pod

1 cinnamon stick

4 cloves

4 fresh bay leaves

2 sprigs of fresh rosemary

3 oranges

3 lemons

Cover the yeast with 100ml of lukewarm water. Melt the butter, then let it cool a bit while you whisk the eggs in a large bowl until pale and fluffy. Still whisking, gradually pour in the melted butter, then the flour, a pinch of sea salt and the yeast mixture, switching to a rubber spatula when it gets too stiff. After 5 minutes it should be thick, smooth and shiny. Cover with a clean damp tea towel and leave in a draught-free place for 40 minutes.

Uncover the baba batter and mix vigorously for 3 minutes so it's loose and shiny. Generously butter a deep 24cm Bundt tin and pour in the batter. Prove again, uncovered, for a further 40 minutes, or until the batter sits just above the edge of the tin. Preheat the oven to 150°C.

Gently place the baba in the oven for 1 hour, or until golden. Meanwhile, for the syrup, place the sugar and limoncello in a pan. Split the vanilla pod lengthways and add with the cinnamon, cloves, bay and rosemary. Use a speed-peeler to add strips of peel from the oranges and lemons, then squeeze all their juice into a measuring jug. Top up to 500ml with water, then pour into the pan. Boil and reduce by half to a syrupy consistency.

Leave the baba to cool, then put your knife at the tin's edge and trim off the excess sponge (perfect in my Limoncello tiramisù on page 342). Gradually feed the sponge with the syrup, making sure you get down the sides, then leave overnight. The next day, release it on to a cake stand or platter. I like to fill the hole with sweetened ricotta, mascarpone or even ice cream, top with seasonal berries and dust with icing sugar before serving.

CALORIES	FAT	SAT FAT	PROTEIN	CARBS	SUGAR	SALT	FIBRE
446kcal	14.4g	7.6g	7.8g	55.4g	27.6g	0.5g	1.2g

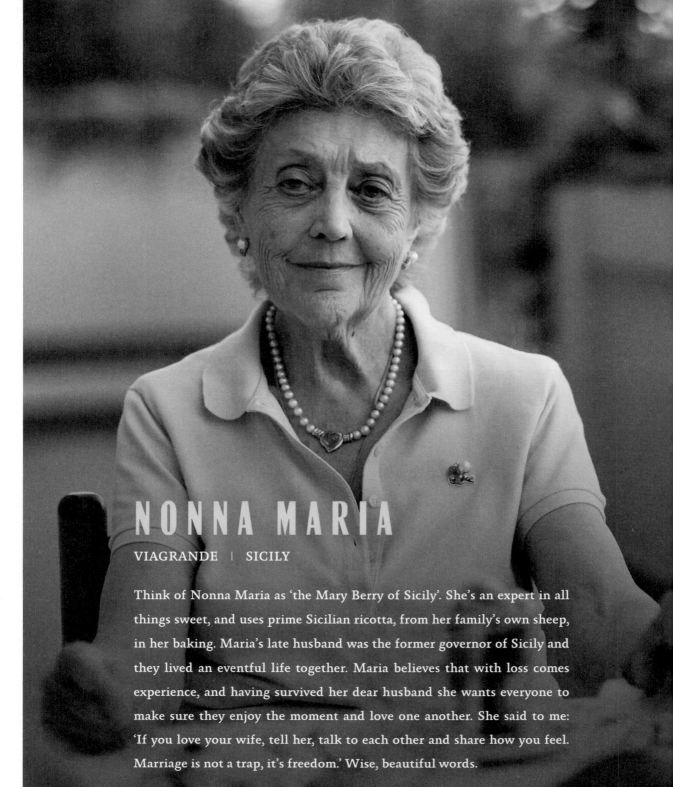

NONNA MARIA

VIAGRANDE | SICILY

Think of Nonna Maria as 'the Mary Berry of Sicily'. She's an expert in all things sweet, and uses prime Sicilian ricotta, from her family's own sheep, in her baking. Maria's late husband was the former governor of Sicily and they lived an eventful life together. Maria believes that with loss comes experience, and having survived her dear husband she wants everyone to make sure they enjoy the moment and love one another. She said to me: 'If you love your wife, tell her, talk to each other and share how you feel. Marriage is not a trap, it's freedom.' Wise, beautiful words.

ROLLED CASSATA

PISTACHIO MARZIPAN, APRICOT JAM & SWEET RICOTTA

~~~~~~

The Arabic influence in Sicilian desserts really sings out in this cassata of silky smooth ricotta with chunks of nuts and chocolate, all wrapped up in Vin Santo sponge and pistachio marzipan. I love this rolled version.

SERVES 16 | 1 HOUR 30 MINUTES, PLUS CHILLING

3 large eggs

100g golden caster sugar

75g plain flour

1 teaspoon vanilla bean paste

unsalted butter, for greasing

100g shelled pistachios

500g white marzipan

icing sugar, for dusting

FILLING

400g quality ricotta cheese

1 tablespoon caster sugar

50g whole hazelnuts

1 heaped tablespoon glacé
   fruit

20g shelled unsalted pistachios

100g dark chocolate (70%)

3 tablespoons apricot jam

50ml Vin Santo

15 glacé cherries

Preheat the oven to 180°C. For the sponge, whisk the eggs and sugar with an electric mixer, or by hand, until pale, fluffy and at least doubled in size. Sift in the flour, add the vanilla paste, then slowly fold through. Grease a baking tray (26cm x 36cm) with butter, then line it with greaseproof paper and grease that, too. Spoon the batter into the tray and bake for 12 to 15 minutes, or until cooked through. Meanwhile, blitz the pistachios in a food processor until fine. Break in the marzipan and blitz until it forms a dough, adding a splash of water to combine, if needed.

Take the sponge out of the oven and confidently flip it out on to a clean tea towel. Peel off the greaseproof, place it back on top, then roll up while the sponge is still warm and flexible. Leave to cool for around 20 minutes.

For the filling, whiz the ricotta with the sugar in a food processor until smooth. Toast the hazelnuts in a frying pan until golden, then finely chop with the glacé fruit, pistachios and chocolate. Mix into the ricotta.

Roll out most of the marzipan on a large sheet of greaseproof paper to 26cm x 46cm, and 2mm thick. Spread over the jam, unroll the sponge on top, drizzle over the Vin Santo and spread over the ricotta. Line up the cherries along the side nearest you, then, using the paper to help you, roll it up, pressing lightly to seal. Trim the ends, then roll out the remaining marzipan and stamp out shapes to decorate the top. Serve it after 30 minutes' chilling in the fridge, or freeze for another day. If frozen, defrost in the fridge for 3 hours before serving. Dust with icing sugar to finish.

CALORIES	FAT	SAT FAT	PROTEIN	CARBS	SUGAR	SALT	FIBRE
189kcal	8.4g	3.3g	5.2g	24.2g	16.1g	0.1g	0.5g

SEMIFREDDO

VANILLA, VIN SANTO & CANTUCCI

~~~~~~

Ice-cream lovers rejoice! Semifreddo (semi-frozen) could be your new best friend – it allows you to celebrate all that you love about ice cream, but gives you the ability to achieve fantastic results without an ice-cream machine. Enjoy a scoop of this super-classy, delicious dessert on its own or alongside a warm tasty tart.

SERVES 10 | 50 MINUTES, PLUS FREEZING

750ml Vin Santo

5 large eggs

500ml double cream

2 tablespoons caster sugar

1 tablespoon vanilla bean paste

cantucci, amaretti or biscotti biscuits, to serve

Place a 30cm serving dish in the freezer to get cold. Pour the Vin Santo into a large pan on a high heat and reduce for about 20 minutes, or until slightly thickened and just coating the back of a spoon. Leave to cool, during which time it will naturally thicken a little more. Meanwhile, get three large clean bowls. Separate the eggs, putting the whites into one bowl and the yolks into another, and pour the cream into the third.

Whisk the egg yolks with the sugar until doubled in volume. With a super-clean whisk, whip the egg whites and a pinch of sea salt until stiff. Finally, add the vanilla paste to the cream and whisk into silky, delicate, soft peaks – don't over-whip. Gently fold the egg whites, egg yolks and half the Vin Santo syrup into the cream, turning the bowl as you go and folding the mixture from the outside in with a gentle finesse to retain as much earnt air as possible. Transfer to your frozen serving dish, ripple lightly with half the remaining syrup and freeze for at least 3 hours, or until set.

I normally move my semifreddo from freezer to fridge about 30 minutes before serving, giving a scoopable dessert ready to dish up. To serve, drizzle over the remaining syrup, then smash and crumble over the biscuits. A little extra glass of Vin Santo for sipping will always go down a treat, too.

CALORIES	FAT	SAT FAT	PROTEIN	CARBS	SUGAR	SALT	FIBRE
374kcal	30g	17.5g	4.5g	9.3g	9.3g	0.2g	0g

PEAR & HAZELNUT TART

SWEET ORANGE & VANILLA PASTRY

~~~~~~

Hazelnuts are a fantastic swap for almonds in a frangipane tart: one of my favourite ways to celebrate seasonal fruit. With orange- and vanilla-scented crunchy pastry to hold it all together, you've got the perfect trio.

SERVES 12 | 1 HOUR 50 MINUTES

2 oranges

275g unsalted butter (cold)

250g plain flour, plus extra
   for dusting

50g icing sugar

1 teaspoon vanilla bean paste

3 large eggs

olive oil

150g blanched hazelnuts

150g golden caster sugar

3 firm pears

To make the pastry, finely grate the zest of 1 orange into a food processor, add 125g of butter, the flour, icing sugar, vanilla paste and 1 egg, then pulse until it comes together into a ball of dough. Wrap in clingfilm and pop into the fridge to chill for 30 minutes. Lightly oil a 25cm non-stick loose-bottomed tart tin. Preheat the oven to 180°C.

On a flour-dusted surface, roll out the pastry to about 3mm thick, then loosely roll it up around the rolling pin and unroll over the oiled tin, easing and pushing it carefully into the sides. Trim off any excess and patch up any holes. Line with a double layer of non-PVC clingfilm, then fill with uncooked rice. Bake blind for 15 minutes. Remove the clingfilm and rice, bake for a further 5 minutes, then leave to cool.

For the frangipane, blitz the nuts into a fine powder in the food processor. Add the remaining 150g of butter and the caster sugar and blitz again to combine. Finely grate in the remaining orange zest, crack in the remaining 2 eggs and blitz again. Just before assembling, peel the pears, quarter lengthways and remove the cores, then toss in the juice of half an orange.

Spoon the frangipane into the pastry case in an even layer, then arrange the pear quarters on top. Bake at the bottom of the oven for 40 minutes, or until golden. Leave for 5 minutes in the tin, then release and serve warm. Nice with orange-spiked crème fraîche and crumbled toasted hazelnuts.

CALORIES	FAT	SAT FAT	PROTEIN	CARBS	SUGAR	SALT	FIBRE
428kcal	28.6g	13g	5.8g	39.5g	23.3g	0.1g	2.7g

RICE PUDDING SEMIFREDDO

MARSALA FIGS SPIKED WITH ORANGE, BAY & VANILLA

Rice pudding ice cream is one of my favourite things, so it feels like a wonderful opportunity to share this semifreddo recipe, which makes it possible for anyone to recreate the vibe at home. It's fantastic with these Marsala figs, but you can choose any seasonal fruit – strawberries, apricots, cherries, plums, you name it.

SERVES 8 | 1 HOUR 10 MINUTES, PLUS COOLING & FREEZING

1.2 litres whole milk

2 vanilla pods

2 fresh bay leaves

1 cinnamon stick

1 orange

150g Arborio risotto rice

4 large eggs

150g golden caster sugar

200ml double cream

8 figs

100ml Marsala wine

Pour the milk into a casserole pan and place on a very low heat. Split 1 vanilla pod lengthways, scrape out the seeds and add both pod and seeds to the pan with 1 bay leaf and the cinnamon. Peel in 3 strips of orange peel with a speed-peeler, stir in the rice and simmer for 1 hour, or until the rice is tender, thick and creamy, stirring occasionally. Pick out the bay leaf, orange peel, cinnamon and vanilla pod, mash about half of the rice, stirring it back through for mega creaminess, then pour into a deep oval freezerproof serving dish and leave to cool completely.

Separate the eggs. Whisk the yolks with 100g of the sugar until pale and fluffy. In separate bowls, with a super-clean whisk, whip the whites, then the cream until they form stiff peaks. Stir the yolks into the cooled rice, fold through the cream, then the whites. Cover and freeze for 6 hours, or until set, beating twice during that time. Eat now, or you can leave it overnight, just move it from freezer to fridge 30 minutes to 1 hour before you want to eat so you have a semi-frozen, scoopable dessert.

To serve, halve the figs and place in a frying pan on a medium heat with the remaining sugar and bay leaf, and the Marsala. Split the remaining vanilla pod lengthways, scrape out the seeds and add both pod and seeds to the pan. Strip in the remaining orange zest and squeeze in the juice. Boil, then simmer gently for 20 minutes, turning the figs halfway. Remove from the heat and cool, then serve alongside the semifreddo.

CALORIES	FAT	SAT FAT	PROTEIN	CARBS	SUGAR	SALT	FIBRE
376kcal	16g	8.9g	10.6g	48.1g	32.2g	0.3g	1g

GRANITA

HOMEMADE ALMOND MILK, COFFEE & BLACKBERRY

~~~~~~

The original granita was celebrated by street vendors, who obtained massive blocks of ice from the mountains in winter and kept them in cold houses through to the summer, when they would scrape delicate shards of ice off the blocks and toss them with sugar and lemon juice to create the ultimate palate refresher. Many hundreds of years later, I enjoyed the most incredible granita of my life, a long way from the ice-capped mountains, on the Aeolian island of Salina with Alfredo. That moment has inspired these delightful recipes.

EACH SERVES 8-10 | EACH TAKES 10-20 MINUTES, PLUS SOAKING OR COOLING & FREEZING

HOMEMADE ALMOND MILK   Place **500g of blanched almonds** in a bowl, cover by 5cm with water and leave to soak overnight. The next day, in a food processor, blitz the almonds and 800ml of their soaking water with **3 tablespoons of runny honey** and a pinch of sea salt until fine (you may need to work in batches). Push the mixture through a sieve, then stir 300g of the pulp from the sieve back through to create great texture (you can freeze the remaining pulp in ice cube trays and add it to porridge or creamy curries).

COFFEE   Sweeten **1 litre of strong quality coffee** (the flavour will lessen when frozen) to taste with **1 teaspoon of vanilla bean paste** and up to **4 tablespoons of runny honey**, then leave to cool.

BLACKBERRY   In a food processor, blitz **800g of frozen wild blackberries** with **3 tablespoons of runny honey** and 200ml of water until smooth, then push the mixture through a sieve to remove the seeds.

METHOD   Tip your chosen mixture into a wide, shallow freezerproof container and freeze – the almond and blackberry will need 2 hours, and the coffee 4 hours. When the time's up, scratch into ice crystals with a fork to your desired consistency. Now, freeze for a further 2 to 3 hours, scratching with a fork every 30 minutes (the coffee granita is naturally harder to scratch), then serve. Each flavour is delicious in its own right, but I love to pair the almond one with the coffee or the blackberry, as it complements them so well. If making ahead, take out of the freezer to thaw for 15 minutes, then break up and blitz in a food processor.

THESE VALUES ARE AN AVERAGE OF THE THREE RECIPES ABOVE

CALORIES	FAT	SAT FAT	PROTEIN	CARBS	SUGAR	SALT	FIBRE
113kcal	7g	0.6g	3g	9.8g	9.3g	0.1g	0g

BASICS

OOZY POLENTA

BUTTERY, CHEESY, STODGY DELICIOUSNESS

Polenta is one of the foundations of cucina povera – cheap energy food that can be served wet like mashed potato, or cooked until firm and set, then cut up and roasted, fried or grilled. This simple but robust ingredient can be used in so many different ways, whether served with stews, braised or roasted meats and fish, or even as starter plates with pan-fried scallops, prawns or squid on top. There's no limit to the ways you can enjoy it.

SERVES 8-10 | 45 MINUTES

400g coarse polenta

100g Parmesan cheese

100g unsalted butter

Bring 2 litres of salted water to the boil over a medium heat, then gradually add the coarse polenta, whisking constantly to prevent lumps. Simmer gently for 40 minutes, stirring regularly with a wooden spoon (you can get quick-cook polenta that's ground much finer, but I don't think it tastes as nice). The polenta is ready when it comes easily away from the edge of the pan – you want a thick consistency. Turn the heat off, finely grate the Parmesan and stir in with the butter. If your polenta thickens too much, add splashes of boiling water to loosen it to the consistency you like. Taste, season to perfection with sea salt and black pepper, then serve.

Now, normally in the base of the pan there's a layer of crispy polenta that sticks, almost like a giant taco. This is a cook's treat – don't tell anyone about it, it's just for you. Use a fish slice to scrape the crispy polenta off the pan, place on a plate, drizzle with good oil, add a fine grating of Parmesan and some chopped fresh chilli, then devour in a quiet corner.

If you want to make this in advance, simply place the finished polenta in a heatproof bowl, cover, then sit it over very gently simmering water, where it will keep warm very happily for up to 2 hours, without compromise.

CALORIES	FAT	SAT FAT	PROTEIN	CARBS	SUGAR	SALT	FIBRE
323kcal	14.2g	9.2g	8g	39.9g	0.4g	0.6g	1.5g

ROYAL PASTA DOUGH

FOR THE SILKIEST, VELVETY PASTA

~~~~~~

Made with a simple blend of Tipo 00 flour (00 means it's super-fine) and fine semolina, which has wonderful flavour and a golden colour, as well as free-range egg yolks, this is my ultimate fresh pasta dough recipe.

SERVES 8 | 30 MINUTES, PLUS RESTING

THE DOUGH Pile **400g of Tipo 00 flour** and **75g of fine semolina** into a large bowl and make a well in the middle. Separate **12 large eggs** and add the yolks to the well (freeze the egg whites in a sandwich bag for making meringues another day). Add **2 tablespoons of extra virgin olive oil** and 4 tablespoons of cold water to the well, use a fork to whip up with the yolks until smooth, then gradually bring the flour in from the outside until it becomes too hard to mix. Get your floured hands in there and bring it together into a ball of dough, then knead on a flour-dusted surface for 4 minutes, or until smooth and elastic (eggs can vary in size and flour can vary in humidity; this dough shouldn't be too wet or dry, but tweak with a touch more water or flour if you need to – use your common sense). Wrap in clingfilm and leave to relax for 30 minutes.

ROLLING OUT Divide your pasta dough into 4 pieces, covering everything with a clean damp tea towel as you go to stop it drying out. You can either roll it out to your desired thickness with a rolling pin, or I think it's more accurate and fun to use a pasta machine, in which case attach it firmly to a clean table.

STAGE 1 One at a time, flatten each piece of dough by hand and run it through the thickest setting, then take the rollers down two settings and run the dough through again to make it thinner. Importantly, fold it in half and run it back through the thickest setting again – I like to repeat this a few times because it makes the dough super-smooth and turns it from a tatty sheet into one that fills out the pasta machine properly.

STAGE 2 Start rolling the sheet down through each setting, dusting with flour as you go. Turn the crank with one hand while the other maintains just a little tension to avoid any kinks, folds or ripples. On a flour-dusted surface, take it right down to the desired thickness. Generally speaking you want about 2mm for shapes like linguine, tagliatelle and lasagne, then to go as thin as 1mm for anything turned into a filled pasta, because when it's folded around a filling it will double up to 2mm. And remember, some shapes are easier than others, but with a bit of patience and practice, you'll soon get the hang of it. Have fun!

CALORIES	FAT	SAT FAT	PROTEIN	CARBS	SUGAR	SALT	FIBRE
373kcal	17.3g	3.9g	13.7g	41.1g	0.8g	0.1g	1.6g

HERO TOMATO SAUCE

SWEET CHERRY TOMATOES, GARLIC, CHILLI & BASIL

~~~~~~

By using top-quality tinned cherry tomatoes, which have a wonderful natural sweetness, you're able to achieve a truly elegant and vivacious sauce that really sings of summer but can be made all year round. One taste, and you'll be transported back to warm summer nights in Italy – you can't argue with that! This sauce works really well for lots of recipes in this book, like my Gnudi (see page 182) and Pizza fritta (see page 306), and to be honest, I just like to make a batch when I have time, ready to use in all kinds of dishes in the days that follow. It's a great freezer staple, and a recipe I hope you'll come back to again and again. Enjoy.

MAKES APPROX. 1 LITRE | 20 MINUTES

4 cloves of garlic

olive oil

2 fresh red chillies

1 big bunch of fresh basil (60g)

4 x 400g tins of quality cherry tomatoes

Peel and finely slice the garlic and place in a large pan on a medium heat with 2 tablespoons of oil. Fry until lightly golden, stirring occasionally, while you halve the chillies lengthways (deseed if you like) and stir into the pan. Tear in the basil (stalks and all). Scrunch in the tomatoes through your clean hands, then swirl a little water around each tin and pour into the pan. Bring the whole lot to the boil, then simmer for 10 to 15 minutes.

Remove the pan from the heat, and now you've got a choice – you can either leave the sauce chunky, or I like to pass it through a coarse sieve, making sure to really push all that goodness through. Taste, season to perfection with sea salt and black pepper, and you're done. You can use the sauce straight away, cover and keep it in the fridge for up to 1 week, or divide between ziplock bags, label and freeze in portions for future meals.

THESE VALUES ARE BASED ON 100G

CALORIES	FAT	SAT FAT	PROTEIN	CARBS	SUGAR	SALT	FIBRE
42kcal	2.5g	0.4g	1.4g	3.8g	3.2g	0.1g	0.7g

GARLIC AÏOLI

SILKY, PUNGENT, PEPPERY & DELICIOUS

It's a joy to partake in the ritual of making a good aïoli. The process has broken many a cook – not because it's hard or complicated, but because it's an emulsification of oil and egg yolk: add too much oil too quickly and it can easily split – this method demands focus. So why do it? Most shop-bought mayo, which would be the base, doesn't use good oil, so here you have the power to make something lip-smackingly special. An aïoli is similar to a mayonnaise, but it's pungent and almost spicy with the hum of raw garlic. It's a boisterous condiment that, when made well and used in the right dish with restraint, is phenomenal. When a blob hits a hot soup, what might be too much in its raw state mingles to become something fantastic, and, when a small spoonful is rubbed across hot toast with cold roasted meats or dressed crab and a little lemon, you'll discover a whole new level of deliciousness. So treat it more like Tabasco or English mustard, just like an antagonist.

MAKES 1 JAR | 25 MINUTES

2 large eggs

100ml cold-pressed extra
   virgin olive oil

300ml mild olive oil

1 lemon

1 clove of garlic

Separate the eggs (save the whites for another recipe), placing the yolks in a large bowl. Scrunch up a wet cloth and place it on your surface so you can sit the bowl at an angle without it slipping. Adding it a drip at a time so you don't split the yolks, whisk in the extra virgin olive oil, then the olive oil, speeding up the drips as you go – when it starts to really thicken, add a squeeze of lemon juice to loosen, then continue adding the oil, with more lemon when needed, use your instincts. Season to taste, tweaking with more lemon, if needed. To up the pepperiness, add more extra virgin olive oil, or add olive oil to make it milder. This gives you a nice base.

Now, peel the garlic and smash it up in a pestle and mortar with a small pinch of salt, then stir it through to create a feisty aïoli, ready to use in lots of different dishes. Sometimes I add an extra flavour, depending on the dish I'm serving it with, making aïoli continually exciting to use. Try smashing up and whisking in 4 anchovy fillets, adding flecks of finely chopped or smashed fresh soft herbs, stirring through chopped fresh chilli, to taste, or even a little saffron that you've steeped in boiling water.

THESE VALUES ARE BASED ON 1 TABLESPOON

CALORIES	FAT	SAT FAT	PROTEIN	CARBS	SUGAR	SALT	FIBRE
246kcal	27g	4g	0.5g	0.1g	0g	0g	0g

SIMPLE PESTOS

Pesto can be made with any combination of herbs and nuts, but here's four of my own personal favourites: basil & pine nut, myrtle & walnut, parsley & hazelnut, rocket & almond. Whichever pairing you go for, pick the leaves from **1 bunch of fresh herbs (30g)** into a pestle and mortar and bash to a paste with a pinch of sea salt. Peel and bash in **1 small clove of garlic**, then pound in **100g of your chosen nuts** until fine. Muddle in **6 tablespoons of extra virgin olive oil**, finely grate in **50g of pecorino or Parmesan cheese**, squeeze in the juice from just **¼ of a lemon**, stir, season to perfection, and tweak to your liking. Bellissimo!

PRESERVED TOMATOES

THE TASTE OF SUMMERTIME, BOTTLED

You might wonder whether this is worth doing when you can buy great tinned tomatoes – the answer is a big yes! Think of this as a lovely process that allows you to create something amazing and vivacious from tomatoes. When they're ripe and delicious, whether you grow your own and have a glut, or when there are boxes available at the end of the day at your local veg market being sold off ripe and cheap, that's the moment to preserve your own in glass jars or bottles. This wonderful treat can kiss any stew, sauce or pasta dish with the vibrant flavours of summertime – sweet, fresh and with the taste of how greenhouses smell.

MAKES 6 JARS | 45 MINUTES, PLUS STERILIZING & COOLING

Get yourself a load of clean glass jars with sealable lids (to give you a guide, around **2kg of ripe tomatoes** will fill about 6 regular jam jars). Give your big batch of tomatoes a wash, then remove all the stalks. Depending on the size of your jars, either halve or quarter the tomatoes, then start stuffing them into the jars, intermittently adding a leaf of **fresh basil**, a slice of **peeled garlic** and a little pinch of seasoning. The bulk of the preserved tomatoes I make will follow the process above, but I also like to add extra flavour to a few jars. Interspersed **anchovy fillets** melt away and add a lovely depth of flavour, or sometimes I add **sliced fresh chilli** for a bit of heat. If I'm growing different coloured tomatoes, I like to keep the colours in separate jars.

Now, use the handle of a wooden spoon to push and compress everything, making sure the jars are well packed – it's important to avoid any gaps, so add more tomatoes, if needed. Once full, add a drizzle of **olive oil** to seal each jar, then screw the lids on tightly. Submerge the jars in a large pan of gently boiling water, then boil for 30 minutes to lightly cook the tomatoes and sterilize the jars. Turn the heat off and leave to cool overnight in the water. These will keep for up to 3 months in a cool, dark place. Once opened, keep in the fridge and use within a week. Trust me, once you taste them, they won't last long!

THESE VALUES ARE BASED ON 100G

CALORIES	FAT	SAT FAT	PROTEIN	CARBS	SUGAR	SALT	FIBRE
17kcal	0.3g	0.1g	0.7g	3.1g	3.1g	0.1g	1g

OLIVE OIL PASTRY

FLAKY, CRUNCHY & LIGHT

~~~~~~

Making pastry with olive oil is very common in the hotter parts of the Mediterranean. You can use it in sweet or savoury recipes; it's very simple to make, feels lighter than regular butter pastry, and while it can fall apart more easily, being rustic it is easy to patch it back together. You can even grate or slice it if needed, to push it into the shape of whatever mould you're using – this is a more amateur technique but I really like it.

MAKES APPROX. 1.5KG | 10 MINUTES, PLUS CHILLING

1kg Tipo 00 flour, plus extra
  for dusting

optional: ½ teaspoon golden
  caster sugar

4 large eggs

200ml mild olive oil

100ml extra virgin olive oil

Pour the flour into a large bowl with a good pinch of sea salt and – if you're making a sweet recipe – the sugar. Make a well in the middle, crack in the eggs, then pour in both oils and 120ml of warm water. Use a fork to whip up the wet mixture, gradually bringing the flour in from the outside until it comes together as a rough ball of dough.

Tip on to a clean surface and knead for just a couple of minutes, then wrap in clingfilm and place in the fridge for at least 1 hour before use, where it will keep well for a couple of days. Or you can even line pastry moulds and freeze them, ready to cook from frozen. To roll out, simply use a rolling pin to get the pastry to your desired thickness on a lightly floured surface, or use the more rustic push-and-shape technique I described in the intro.

THESE VALUES ARE BASED ON 100G

CALORIES	FAT	SAT FAT	PROTEIN	CARBS	SUGAR	SALT	FIBRE
630kcal	32.4g	4.8g	16.8g	67.9g	1.8g	0.3g	2.6g

PREPARING ARTICHOKES

Prepping artichokes is a wonderfully brilliant, thoughtful ritual to partake in and, I find, a very calming process. The instructions below will help you prepare Italian violet artichokes, which I use throughout this book. Also, if you have a plot of land, growing artichokes is beyond easy, they look extraordinary and their yield is pretty high. Bearing in mind they can be expensive to buy, growing your own could be win–win. Try and give your artichokes a little squeeze before you buy them to check they're nice and firm and at their best.

Squeeze the juice from a few lemons into a big bowl of cold water, dropping the squeezed lemon halves into the bowl as you go, but keeping 1 halved lemon out so you can use it to rub the artichokes as you prep them. Artichokes oxidize and discolour super-quickly once exposed to air, so it's important to rub them with acid as you go, keeping them submerged in lemon water thereafter.

One artichoke at a time, click off the outer leaves – about half in total – until you get to the paler, yellowy-white, more tender ones. With a sharp knife, trim 5cm below and above the base of the choke, rubbing the exposed cuts with lemon as you go. Use a small sharp knife or speed-peeler to peel the base and stalk, revealing the soft flesh underneath. Rub it all over with one of your lemon halves.

Get a teaspoon, insert it into the middle of the leaves, then turn and scrape it to remove the inner, fluffy choke – look inside to check you've done an accurate job. Once done, simply squeeze in some lemon juice.

At this point you can use them whole, halve or quarter them as your recipe calls for, or, of course, slice, dice or do whatever you want with them! The possibilities are endless.

FLAVOURED SALT

HERBS, SPICES, CHILLI, LEMON & PORCINI

Local seasonings are common around Italy. Italians tend to use whatever spices and herbs are abundant locally, blending them with salt to create the most incredible flavour-packed seasoning. You'll find these mixes often define the key flavours of the region. As well as being delicious, flavouring salt means you get a bigger bang for your buck, so you'll end up using less salt, which can only be a good thing in my book.

MAKES 1 JAR | 15 MINUTES, PLUS DRYING

1 heaped teaspoon caraway
    seeds

1 tablespoon white
    peppercorns

1 tablespoon fennel seeds

6 cloves

4 dried red chillies

2 tablespoons dried oregano,
    ideally the flowering kind

20g dried porcini mushrooms

1 clove of garlic

1 lemon

2 fresh bay leaves

400g sea salt

Put the dried spices, chillies, oregano and porcini into a blender and blitz until fine. Peel and add the garlic, then finely grate in the lemon zest, add the bay leaves and blitz again. Blitz in the sea salt, taking the texture as fine as you can – you may need to work in batches, and it might help to stop halfway to mix things up with a rubber spatula. Tip on to a tray and leave to dry overnight, or in the sun, until hard and crunchy.

The next day, smash it together, push it through a coarse sieve so you're just left with a powder, then decant into a jar (I usually put a few small grains of rice at the bottom first to help absorb any excess moisture).

THESE VALUES ARE BASED ON 1 TEASPOON

CALORIES	FAT	SAT FAT	PROTEIN	CARBS	SUGAR	SALT	FIBRE
1kcal	0g	0g	0.1g	0.1g	0g	3.4g	0g

HOW TO JOINT A CHICKEN

1 Break the knuckles and chop them off with a sharp knife, through the joint.

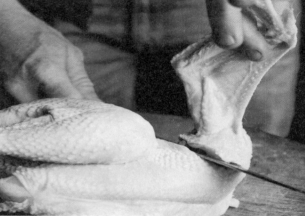

2 Pull out the wings and cut them off at the base, cutting slightly into the breast so you get a generous meaty portion.

3 Lightly cut through the skin between the chicken leg and breast, so that the leg falls to the side.

4 Bend the leg backwards to disjoint it, and turn breast side down.

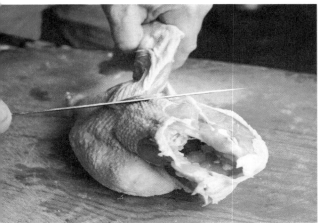

5 Cut between the leg and breast, removing the whole leg, then repeat.

6 Find the joint in between the drumstick and thigh, tap the heel of the knife and cut through the bone, separating the drumstick and thigh, then repeat.

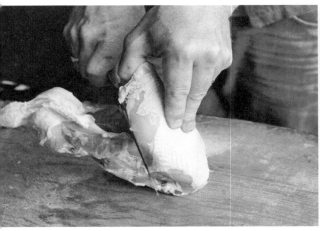

7 Leaving the breasts on the bone, carefully cut between the breasts and the backbone to separate the front and back of the bird.

8 Slice between the breasts on the bone to separate, then use the heel of the knife to cut across each breast through the bone, giving two large chunks.

A NOTE FROM JAMIE'S NUTRITION TEAM

'Our job is to make sure that Jamie can be super-creative, while also ensuring that all his recipes meet the guidelines we set. Every book has a different brief, and *Jamie Cooks Italy* is a real celebration of Italian cuisine, focusing both on meals you can enjoy every day, and on more indulgent food for weekends and special occasions. So that you can make clear, informed choices, we've published the nutritional content for each recipe on the actual recipe page itself, giving you a really easy access point to understand how to fit these recipes into your week. You know the score – a good, balanced, varied diet and regular exercise are the keys to a healthier lifestyle. For more info about how we analyse recipes, please visit jamieoliver.com/nutrition.'

Rozzie Batchelar, Senior Nutritionist, RNutr (food)

FOOD STANDARDS, FREEZING & OVEN TEMPERATURES

I think there's no point in eating meat unless the animal was raised well, was free to roam, lived in an unstressful environment and was in great health. It makes total sense that what we put into our bodies is optimal in every way, to in turn give us maximum goodness. I also think that we should all be striving to eat way more plant-based meals that hero veg, beans and pulses, and enjoying better-quality meat, less often. With this in mind, please choose organic, free-range or higher-welfare meat whenever you can, making sure beef or lamb is grass-fed. The same goes for eggs and anything containing eggs, such as pasta – choose free-range or organic, and please choose organic stock.

When it comes to buying fish, make sure you choose responsibly sourced wherever possible – look for the MSC logo, or talk to your fishmonger or the guys at the fish counter in your local supermarket and take their advice. Try to mix up your choices, choosing seasonal, sustainable options as they're available.

With staple dairy products, like milk, yoghurt and butter, I couldn't endorse more the trade-up to organic. It is slightly more expensive, but we're talking pennies not pounds, so this is a much easier trade-up than with meat. Plus, every time you buy organic, you really are voting for a better food system.

Finally, to help elevate your Italian dishes to their maximum potential, I'd strongly recommend buying the best-quality olive oils, capers, tinned or jarred anchovies, tinned tomatoes and stone-in olives you can get your hands on – you definitely get what you pay for where these ingredients are concerned.

Let food cool before freezing, breaking it down into portions so it cools quicker and you can get it into the freezer within 2 hours of cooking. Make sure everything is well wrapped, meat and fish especially, and labelled up for future reference. Thaw in the fridge before use. Generally, if you've frozen cooked food, don't freeze it again after you've reheated it.

Recipes are tested in fan-assisted ovens. You can find conversions for conventional ovens, °F and gas online.

HUNGRY FOR MORE?

For handy nutrition advice, as well as videos, features, hints, tricks and tips on all sorts of different subjects, loads of brilliant recipes, plus much more, check out

JAMIEOLIVER.COM

GRAZIE

I've been working on this beautiful book, and the TV show that accompanies it, for the past 18 months. It's been a painstaking labour of love and so many people have helped me out on my journey, both in Italy and back here in the UK during the physical creation of the book. It's simply not possible for me to list everyone here, but you can see just a handful of the wonderful characters I've met on the pages before this one.

Me and the team have experienced great hospitality and friendship wherever we've travelled, whether it's to visit old friends or new. I must give a particular mention to my dear friends in Tuscany, Luca St Just at Petrolo, Giovanni Manetti at Fontodi, and the incredible Mr Dario Cecchino, as well as my stylish brother-in-law Salvatore Cimmino, who helped us to make many introductions in Naples, and beyond.

Hopefully throughout this book you've enjoyed reading about some of the incredibly inspiring nonnas I met, and as well as thanking them for welcoming me with such open arms, I must extend my thanks to their families and their friends, who looked after us, looked after the nonnas, and were all ever so helpful and accommodating wherever we went.

Big love to my family, Jools, Poppy, Daisy, Petal, Buddy and River, for holding the fort when I was away in Italy, and constantly supporting me in all that I do. And of course, lots of love to my wonderful mum and dad, to Anna, and to Mrs Norton and Leon Manzi, too.

To my wonderful food team, some of you have travelled with me to the mountains and the islands, and some of you have helped me test these recipes to the hilt. I'm so grateful for everything that you do, and happy that we could share this epic journey of inspiration. To queen of the gang, Ginny Rolfe – I know it's not easy being away from your babies and having to look after me and Gennaro instead, so thank you. To her gaggle of girls, Abi 'Scottish' Fawcett, Christina 'Boochie' Mackenzie, Maddie Rix, Jodene Jordan, Elspeth Allison, Sophie Mackinnon and Rachel Young – you're all fantastic and well above average. To my Aussie mate Jonny Lake, back in the homeland, and to new star boy in the mix Hugo Harrison – nice one, boys. To the matrix that is Pete Begg and to Bobby Sebire, my loyal soldiers, thanks for all your help, as ever. To Rozzie Batchelar, nutritionist and cake lover, big thanks for everything you do. Without Jo Lewis, Athina Andrelos, Bianca Koffman and Helen Martin, nothing would ever happen – thank you, girls. And big love to extra recipe testers Isla Murray, Becca Sulocki and Pip Spence.

On words, shout out to my ever-patient editor Rebecca 'Rubs' Verity, testing-organization-ninja Beth Stroud and Frances Stewart. You're all amazing and I'm sure I don't deserve you. Thank you for all that you do.

To Mr David Loftus, the photo maestro, thank you for all the epic pictures, mate – both the food and the gorgeous reportage and portraits. The visual pace of this book is stunning, and it's a credit to you.

MILLE!

On the design front, big love to my mate James Verity at creative agency Superfantastic for keeping things fresh and exciting. This is a big book and a lot of work has gone into it – I couldn't be happier. Thank you.

My long-standing publishers, Penguin Random House, headed up by the big boss Mr Tom Weldon, are a constant support. Huge thank you as always to the core team, lovely Louise Moore, tattooed and talented John Hamilton, and amazing Juliette Butler, Nick Lowndes, Elizabeth Smith, Bek Sunley, Clare Parker, Chantal Noel and Chris Turner. And to all the brilliant bods making up their teams, Katherine Tibbals, Annie legendary Lee, Pat Rush, Caroline Pretty, Emma Horton, Caroline Wilding, Stuart Anderson, Jenny Platt, Anjali Nathani, Catherine Wood, Lucy Beresford-Knox, Celia Long, Sarah Davison-Aitkins, Ben Hughes, Lucy Keeler, Rachel Myers, Chris Wyatt, Tracy Orchard, Lee-Anne Williams and Jessica Sacco.

Back on my side, lots of love to the PR and marketing gang, Jeremy Scott, Tamsyn Zietsman, Laura Jones and Natalie Woolfe, and to Subi Gnanaseharam on social. Huge love to my CEO, my dear brother-in-law Paul Hunt, and to epic ladies Louise Holland, Claire Postans, Zoe Collins and Sy Brighton. I don't have space to list everyone from the office, but please don't doubt that I appreciate all that you do to support the book and TV and share the love. To all of my wonderful teams – food, technical, nutrition, editorial, marketing, comms, art, social, digital video, personal, legal, operations, IT, finance, P&D, facilities – you're all amazing!

Now on to TV, which I hope you enjoy watching as much as we enjoyed our travels. On editorial, big shout out to Katy Fryer, Nicola Pointer, Alana Moreno, Katie Millard, Mario Gangarossa and Dave Minchin. On production – and this one's been epic – thanks to Sean Moxhay, Susan Cassidy, Vicky Bennetts and Camilla Cabras. To the crew – boys, we've certainly shared a few special moments during this series – love as always to Dave Miller, Olly Wiggins, Calum Thomson, Richard Shaw, Jonnie Vacher and Rollo Scott. Back to reality and big thanks to the edit gang – Emma Peach, Paul Frost, Simon Beeley, Jessica Parrish, Naz Abdullah, Page Shepherd, Emma Slack, Jamie Mac, Stephen Leigh, Annie Backhouse, Jon Hubbard, Andrew Mckenzie, Joanna Lincoln, Sophie Kennedy and Liz Roe. I have huge appreciation for our Italian fixers and drivers, Alison Ercolani, Maria Laura Frullini, Giuseppe Gallucci, Ermanno Guida, Giorgio Vigna and Santino Rossello. Thank you, as ever, to lovely ladies Julia Bell and Lima O'Donnell.

Over at Channel 4, thank you to Jay Hunt for commissioning this series – I wish you all the luck in the future. Big thank you also to Alex Mahon, Ian Katz, Sarah Lazenby, Kelly Webb-Lamb and Hanna Warren. And lots of love to the amazing Fremantle team for taking the show global.

Finally, thank you to Gennaro Contaldo. He's got a lot of love in this book and it's all completely deserved. I couldn't have done these Italy trips without him, and I will treasure the memories we've made. Love you G.

INDEX

Recipes marked V are suitable for vegetarians

For a quick reference list of all the dairy-free, gluten-free and vegan recipes in this book, please visit:

jamieoliver.com/jamiecooksitaly/reference

BOOKS BY JAMIE OLIVER

PHOTOGRAPHY

David Loftus

DESIGN

James Verity at Superfantastic

MICHAEL JOSEPH

UK | USA | CANADA | IRELAND | AUSTRALIA | INDIA | NEW ZEALAND | SOUTH AFRICA

Michael Joseph is part of the Penguin Random House group of companies,
whose addresses can be found at global.penguinrandomhouse.com

Penguin
Random House
UK

First published 2018

001

Copyright © Jamie Oliver, 2018

Photography copyright © Jamie Oliver Enterprises Limited, 2018

Photography by David Loftus & Jamie Oliver (pages 149, 161, 163, 205, 213, 273, 369)

The moral right of the author has been asserted

Design by Superfantastic

Colour reproduction by Altaimage Ltd

Printed in Germany by Mohn Media

A CIP catalogue record for this book is available from the British Library

ISBN: 978–0–718–18773–6

penguin.co.uk

jamieoliver.com